Praise for *The Happy Homeschooler*

"I have to admit that when I read the title "The Happy Homeschooler: 10 Simple Strategies…" I expected a bit o' fluff to some degree. Because if there's anything I've learned about homeschooling over the decades I've been at it, it's that there's nothing "simple" about it. Like anything else, you (and your kids) get as much out of it as you put into it. And while there are many days when "happy" may not describe a tired out momma, there IS deep joy to be found in learning alongside your kiddos…

Be that as it may, there's nothing trite or trivial by what Tracey Hagerman shares in these pages. In a moment of transparency here, while I whole-heartedly agree with each one of her recommended strategies, I found myself wishing I had done better in some of those same areas, for example, when talking about eating right and getting enough exercise. I love that she encourages moms to "Lead by Example" (ch.2) *without* laying on a dose of "mom guilt." Rather, she gently explains exactly why self-care is oh-so-very important! (Ah, where was she when I was a young and careless homeschool mom?)

By outlining practical ways to "Strategically Plan out Your Year" (ch.4) and "Strengthen Your Support System" (ch.5) she answers both the "Why?" and the "How?" (Super-helpful!) And I love her advice about math studies on pages 49-51!

"Put Your Mind at Ease" (ch. 10) is not only a great lesson for new homeschoolers but also an important reminder for homeschool veterans that we don't always see the fruits of our labors right away. Additionally (and just as important), they are often not of the educational variety but better-related to character development. Those kinds of things take time and happen in the future. *But we still need to persevere!*

Finally, approaching one's career as a home educator from the perspective of a project manager (ch. 9) helps homeschool moms develop skills and accomplishments that set them up for a terrific post-homeschool life as well. Which, now that I'm looking back, is <u>un</u>arguably crucial. 'Cause a momma's life isn't over even when the homeschooling years *are*!

She talks about concepts that you don't often see in homeschool books: the importance of doing your own research… how important it is (both a privilege and responsibility) to gently educate our own family and friends about homeschooling… dealing with negativity/negative people… and finding a mentor, to name a few.

Sprinkled throughout are delightful examples from her own life and other homeschool moms' lives with whom she's been on the journey, making the book very relatable.

A simple read? Perhaps. Pages filled with reminders you will frequently want (and need) to have on-hand down the road? Most definitely!"

—**Pat Fenner**, 25-year homeschooler, blogger,
founder of Breakthrough Homeschooling
and author of six books including *The Empty Homeschooler Nest:
Next Steps for Moms after Homeschooling is Over*

THE Happy HOMESCHOOLER

TEN SIMPLE STRATEGIES TO INCREASE PRODUCTIVITY, FOSTER JOY AND AVOID BURNOUT

Tracey Hagerman

ISBN (paperback): 978-1-9995678-5-9

ISBN (.epub): 978-1-9995678-6-6

ISBN (.mobi): 978-1-9995678-7-3

ISBN (pdf): 978-1-9995678-8-0

THIS BOOK IS DEDICATED TO:

Jonathon, my husband, who supported me
every step of the way. I loved taking the
road less traveled with you by my side!

My children, Kent, Kristy and Brooke who opened my
world to so many new and interesting things. I
cherish every moment of our time together.

My parents, Dennis and Madeleine, who were my first
teachers. I am forever grateful that you instilled in me a
love of learning!

Kim Crampton, my friend since grade three, who has
been there with me through every life stage, including
homeschooling. What an amazing time we have enjoyed! I
treasure your friendship more than you will ever know.

Grace Dunlop, my friend and fellow homeschooler,
who has shown me over and over what it means to
truly give of oneself. You inspire me every day!

Betty Stickl, my homeschooling mentor, who
tirelessly answered my homeschooling questions
over the years. I guarantee that your wisdom did
not fall on deaf ears! I am so glad I met you at
the start of my homeschooling journey.

Jackie Gollé for loving on my youngest daughter, Brooke,
and teaching her how to sew. Your selfless dedication
warms my heart every time I think about all the hours you
spent to make a positive difference in a young girl's life!

The memory of Jennifer Murphy-Hupé, my beautiful
friend, who exemplified every day what it meant to
be a happy homeschooler. I miss you so much!

The many amazing homeschoolers my family
and I met along the way. I always feel so blessed
when I am in your company. What a wonderful
adventure we have enjoyed together!

And to you, the homeschooler who chose this book. May
you find the nuggets of information you need
to truly become a happy homeschooler!

And most especially to Almighty God, my greatest
teacher, who nudged me to write this book.

When you are finished reading

be sure to go to
traceyhagerman.com
to claim your free gift.

TABLE OF CONTENTS

INTRODUCTION

Homeschooling can be the most rewarding experience in the world or the most discouraging. Anyone who has ever researched the life of families who homeschool will quickly identify three types of families. There are those who love homeschooling, those who endure homeschooling and those who are ready to give up.

Today, millions of children around the world are homeschooled. This number is rising in leaps and bounds every year as families discover the amazing benefits of homeschooling. Universities and colleges regularly admit homeschooled students into their programs. The vast majority of homeschoolers go on to finish degrees and find gainful employment. If you are thinking of homeschooling or have been homeschooling for a few or many years, this is encouraging news indeed!

Unfortunately for all the parents who chose to home-school, many end up exhausted, discouraged and over-whelmed. After only a few months or even a couple of years, their daily life becomes a grind as they struggle to perform all of the homeschooling duties along with regular life, such as chores, meals and family obligations. Add to this unmotivated kids, to-do lists so long that they will take a year to tackle, negative family members, and you will quickly discover parents and children falling into the abyss of homeschooling burnout.

THE HAPPY HOMESCHOOLER

If you are just starting out and would like to jumpstart your homeschooling success, you will be elated that you found this book. An added bonus is that it is a very quick and easy read!

If you are already homeschooling and would like to incorporate some innovative techniques to invigorate your homeschooling environment, this book will definitely resonate with you.

Maybe you are homeschooling, but constantly find yourself stressed, fatigued and disheartened. Perhaps you are thinking of giving up homeschooling altogether. Deep down you really do believe homeschooling is the best educational choice for your children, but you are finding yourself wondering how you are going to get through the next day, much less the next week or year of homeschooling. If this is the case, then I urge you to stop whatever it is you are doing right now and read this book. You will not be disappointed!

In *The Happy Homeschooler* you will find ten key strategies that will significantly improve your and your children's homeschooling journey. Through simple tweaks, your frustrations will melt away. You will burst with excitement when you realize that the implementation of a few key actions will garner huge results. You will wonder why you ever thought of giving up on homeschooling.

Becoming a happy homeschooler can mean different things to many people. In the broadest sense, it may mean that your children are progressing academically, emotionally, socially, spiritually and in maturity. Overall, there is a sense of peace, joy, hope and well-being in your family. This does not mean that there are no struggles or difficulties, but rather that at most times there is a sense that things are moving forward at an appropriate pace without undue stress, worry and aggravation.

I tell you these things because over time, as my family implemented the things talked about in this book, we saw significant positive results in our homeschooling. My husband, Jonathon, our three children, Kent, Kristy and Brooke and I found our enjoyment of the homeschooling life skyrocket. Friends, family and acquaintances wanted to know what we were doing to yield such high levels of life satisfaction.

The actions outlined in *The Happy Homeschooler* have been compiled based on four things:

- My observations of hundreds of homeschooling families of varying sizes, with whom I have come into contact as the result of participating in innumerable homeschooling outings, activities, conferences, support meetings and co-ops over 18 years.

- My professional background as a project manager and change management consultant, wherein I applied many of the same key principles to our homeschooling journey.

- The successful outcome of homeschooling my three children from Kindergarten to the completion of grade 12 by implementing the actions outlined in this book. All three of my children went on to higher studies. My son, Kent, is now a software engineer working full time in his field; my middle daughter, Kristy, is an audio engineer working full time in the music industry, and my youngest, Brooke, has just started her third year of university studying Business Administration.

- The fact that, the majority of the time, our family absolutely loved homeschooling, and when we did not, we figured out exactly what to tweak.

I cannot begin to count the number of times I have sat down over coffee with potential, current and long-time homeschoolers to explain what key things made the difference. As these families implemented some of the same vital actions in their own homeschooling environments, they would excitedly report back on the positive and lasting changes, in both their children's and their dispositions towards learning and life in general.

If you desire these things for your family, then I urge you not to wait but to take some time right now and find out how you can revolutionize your homeschool environment. I guarantee that you will be happy you did. In fact, you will probably find your family and friends asking you for your own insider secrets!

If you are struggling in any way and do not want to become the statistic of someone who stops homeschooling—not because you think public or private school is better—but because homeschooling has become much too daunting, then you need to read this book.

I have seen parents chastise themselves by guiltily considering placing their kids in school, but instead hang on for another miserable year of homeschooling. They know something needs to change, but they do not know what it is.

INTRODUCTION

I have spoken with parents who placed their children in school and have felt an overwhelming sense of grief and failure as their children spiralled downwards because it was not a good fit for them. If only they had tried to modify a few key areas first, they could have taken their homeschooling from mediocre to magnificent.

We loved homeschooling. Families that do are easy to spot. The parents are happy, the kids are thriving, and life seems almost too good to be true. Is this truly achievable? What do these parents do that others do not? Observational data supports that they have implemented many of the key actions found in this book. I hope you will too.

Some people take an entire year to plan a wedding. So, why not take an hour or two to revolutionize your child's education by reading through this quick but valuable book? As you journey through *The Happy Homeschooler*, you may be surprised at the simplicity of these actions. I guarantee that you will be even more surprised when you apply them and witness the difference they make.

The power to create an awesome homeschooling experience for you and your family is in your hands. I hope you choose to become another happy homeschooler. Your kids will thank you!

I cannot wait to hear all about it! Please feel free to contact me via my website at http://www.traceyhagerman.com to tell me about your journey as you take simple yet highly effective steps to revitalize your homeschooling experience.

Chapter 1

READ TO YOUR CHILDREN

Okay, we've just started, and I know what you are thinking. You say, of course I'm going to read to my child. What parent doesn't start reading to their children long before they can even talk or walk? Right? I mean, which one of us didn't receive a child's book as a gift for our new baby. Yes, it might have only been a picture or cloth book, or one of my favourites—a Dr. Seuss book—but I think we can all agree that reading to a child is normal, natural and helpful in directing a clear path for our child's ability to understand spoken and written language.

All we have to do is walk into the children's section of a library or book store before we are bombarded with shelves bursting with books of all shapes, sizes and subjects. Thus, I think it is fair to say that most of us share the view that books are extremely important to a child's development. So, of course, we all read to our children.

Perhaps by now you are thinking that you have limited time and are tempted to skip to the next chapter to get to the real meat of this book. But I ask you to be patient a few minutes more as I share with you five key things we instituted in our home that I believe made an incredible impact on our three children's voracious interest in books.

Read Above Your Child's Grade Level

The best way I can explain the importance of reading above your children's grade level is to provide you with a concrete example. When our children were young, I remember by late afternoon, I would feel physically and mentally exhausted after a day of chores, cleaning, taking the children outside, etc. When my husband, Jonathon, walked through the door from work, I was eager for him to take over the care of our children. This allowed me to get supper on the table without the little ones underfoot.

In the same manner, Jonathon would be fatigued from his busy day at work and liked to lay down for a few minutes before supper. We came to a compromise that he would take fifteen minutes to get a cold drink and change before our children would join him on our bed for some reading time.

And this is the genius point that I would like to say was my idea, but instead came from another homeschooler who was speaking at a conference. I wish I could remember who she was so I could give her credit for this awesome idea. She encouraged us to read books to our children that were far beyond what they could read themselves. So when our children Kent, Kristy and Brooke were five, three and a newborn, respectively, I handed my husband *Charlotte's Web*, by E. B. White. This was a chapter book with only a few hand-drawn black and white pictures throughout the entire book.

At this time, not one of our children was reading yet. But, even our baby would settle down when my husband read to them. Kent and Kristy would snuggle beside their dad and listen, completely enraptured by the story. Sometimes they would stop and ask questions, but for the most part, they just listened.

When I would call them for supper, often they would want to continue listening to their dad read, even though they were all very hungry. We always read to them at bedtime as well, but let them choose their books. Inevitably they would usually request that my husband continue to read whatever book he had been reading to them earlier.

Three amazing things developed out of this. The first has to do with our son, Kent, who had a great deal of difficulty initially learning to read. Even after finding some amazing curriculum to help him, he struggled with reading and writing for a number of years. At the end of grade six, we decided to have him complete some standardized testing as we wanted to have a better idea of how he was faring. We were flabbergasted when the testing revealed that he scored in the ninety-ninth percentile for vocabulary and comprehension, despite still struggling with spelling and writing. I do not believe this happened by chance. The only plausible explanation was the daily readings of my husband of material beyond what Kent could read himself. Kent is a voracious reader now and has no recollection, other than what we have told him, of how much he struggled with learning to read.

The second incredible thing that came out of reading above their grade level was when our second child, four-year-old Kristy, and I sat together for the first time to formally teach her to read. I explained a few things to her and then took out a reader that was thirty pages long. Each page had one line of text on it. My desire that first day was to have her read one word from each sentence on each page—things like rat, cat, sat, mat and hat—as these were the first words I had helped her with that day.

Imagine my surprise when I opened the book and she smoothly read the entire thing, without missing a single word on any of the pages. When she finished the last page, she turned to me and said, "Surprise!" I am sure my eyes have never been larger than when I stared back at her and said: "When did you learn to do that?"

Her response floored me. She explained that when my husband was reading—even though he was reading a chapter book either with minimal or no pictures in it—she would lie beside him and follow the words with her eyes. Because this reading time was such a regular occurrence in our house, over time, she inadvertently started recognizing the words. She also explained that sometimes when her baby sister fussed and Daddy had to stop for a few minutes or if he fell asleep (imagine that), she would read ahead in the book. Then when Daddy continued, she would watch for the words she was not sure about. To this day, I can honestly say we did not ever really have to teach Kristy to read.

With our third child, Brooke, her gross motor skills seemed to develop much faster than her speaking ability. Initially, she used very few words in succession, while other children her age and younger were putting full sentences together. As I contemplated having her tested to see if she might need some extra help, she hit her third birthday. All of a sudden, her speech came out in paragraphs.

In addition, because Brooke was always around when we were reading to the other two, if we pulled out a book to read specifically to her, she would be able to recount the story, the characters and the precise scenes in the book. It amazed us how much she remembered. She would ask us to hurry up and get to the good part, which she would describe in vivid detail or she would ask us to read another book because she already knew the outcome of the book we had chosen. This continued for years. It did not matter if these books were novels based on Ancient Egypt or literary classics that her siblings studied three or four years before; somehow, she remembered them. Usually more often than I did.

We clued in pretty quickly that Brooke was an auditory learner. All those unschooled years—where she was not of school-age yet—or those years when I was concerned I was not giving her enough time for school because I was focused on the older two, she was actually taking in the reading times like a gigantic sponge. If you have multiple children and you read to them all together, often your younger ones are definitely learning. Vary the types of books you read and just imagine what they will learn!

Every few years, we had each of our children do some standardized testing. This is something we chose to do as part of our homeschooling. We were able to access the materials through our homeschooling association who could source the materials from a reputable testing organization. In each of my children's cases, they always scored above the 95% percentile for vocabulary and comprehension. I attribute this to regularly reading to them beyond their current reading level.

Read to your children daily. Read books without pictures. Read above their current reading level.

Continue Reading to Your Children Even When They Can Read

Both my husband and I loved reading to our children. There is nothing more satisfying than snuggling up under a warm blanket and entering an imaginary world together. I fondly remember when we discovered Beverly Cleary's three-book series about a little mouse called Ralph. My children could not get enough of little Ralph's adventures as he sped around a hotel on his motorcycle.

Sometimes, at the end of the day, when I was feeling especially tired or when I had already read five chapters and the kitchen mess was still looming, I would long for the day when my children could read on their own. They too did not relish having to wait until Mommy finished the laundry or Daddy finished mowing the lawn before they could return to an exciting world hidden in the pages of a chapter book.

I am thankful that another homeschooling mother farther along on the homeschooling path recommended to us that we continue to read to our children, regardless of their age or reading ability. What? You mean even when they are pre-teens and devouring books by the dozens? Yes. How about when they are teenagers? Yes. Continue to read to and with them.

And so we continued to read. Along with novels of all kinds, we read books on Ancient Greece, calligraphy, engines, Shakespeare, art, science and innumerable historical-based fiction novels. We took turns reading aloud. Again, many of these books were well beyond their reading level. This went on well into their teens.

Eventually, to get in even more time, we borrowed audiobooks from the library and listened over lunch, as we folded laundry or when we took a car trip. We never stopped with books. Each of my children's vocabulary grew as did their ability to grasp topics from so many varied interests.

Continue to read to your children and listen to books regardless of their age and reading ability.

Have Your Children Read Aloud

My eldest son currently participates in a weekly Bible study group. Most of the sessions involve taking turns reading from the Bible before discussing the content. This Bible study group is comprised of a very close-knit group of friends who have known each other for many years, and range in age from 18 to 25 years old. They are all comfortable with each other and are highly intelligent, motivated and capable males. My son shared with me recently that many of them have a difficult time reading aloud. They stutter, stammer and stumble over the words.

Our son indicated that he was very surprised, as he himself struggled with reading for many, many years but now can smoothly read aloud to others. He shared this with me not to be critical of his friends, but because he could not remember at what age we stopped reading aloud and wanted to know. As I reiterated that we never really stopped until maybe his late teens, he nodded his head up and down before claiming how the regular practice of reading aloud makes a huge difference. I cannot agree more.

When our youngest was a teen, she tended to skim over words so quickly she often misinterpreted the meaning. Remembering that she is primarily an auditory learner, I would have her slow down and read the words aloud. It was only by practicing reading aloud whether it was her physics, chemistry or business books, that helped her to really understand and assimilate new material because she could hear the words as well as see them. That worked much better for her.

Whenever we had a babysitter, our children would often read to them, instead of the other way around. If their grandparents came for a visit, they were often treated to a story while my husband and I put supper on the table. We encouraged our older daughter to read to our younger daughter. I have so many precious memories of the two of them, snuggled up on the couch, reading books together.

Have your children read aloud to both themselves and others regularly.

Saturate Your House with Books

Another great thing we did was to thoroughly utilize our local libraries. Every three weeks, we would make a trip to one of our local libraries. Each of us was allowed to check out about fifteen books at a time. We made full use of this privilege and would often be found carting out sixty to seventy books in total.

I have to admit that I felt somewhat guilty taking all of these books out at once. One day our librarian informed us that she loved when we visited because their library never had enough shelf space. So they liked when people checked out a ton of books. I felt like we had won the lottery.

Often we had some books we would request in advance, but for the most part, we would walk down the various aisles of the library and pull out anything that caught our eyes. Maybe I need to back up here and say that I would continually pick books that caught my eye, that I thought my children might enjoy. Within five minutes of entering the library, my children would already have their noses buried in the first or second book they pulled off the shelves.

When we arrived home, I would divide the stack of books among our living room coffee table, side tables and a large wicker basket that sat on the floor beside the couch. I do admit this was somewhat strategic because the living room was the only room in the house where our children were not allowed to have any toys. I found that I needed to keep one room clean and free from toys and crafts. I admit this was for my sanity, as I function best with order and tidiness.

After dinner, my husband and I would often take a cup of tea and sit in the living room. As our children loved being with their dad at the end of the day, they would follow us. Since there were only books in the living room, they would naturally pick through the books, and spend a great deal of time reading and flipping through them. And just like that, once again, they would be reading books on new and interesting topics. Three weeks later, we would go back to the library and haul back another massive stack of books.

Did they read all of them? No. Did they read many of them? Yes. Plus, it became clear pretty fast where their interests lay. So on the subsequent visit to the library, I would try to supplement with books I knew would pique their interests.

I remember one particular day when I kept calling my son for supper. When he continued to ignore my requests, I marched into his room and found him sprawled out on his bed reading a book. Without thinking, I found myself threatening to take away his reading privileges for a week. He raced into the kitchen faster than the time a nasty wasp was chasing him up the front steps of our house. Mission accomplished!

Saturate your house with so many books, your friends and neighbours will think you bought out the local book store. Change them often, so they will continue to draw your children to them.

Choose Books over Movies, Television and Electronics

Yes, we are one of those strange families who rarely watched television. Movie night was once every week or two, and we never purchased any gaming devices of any kind. Our children did not have phones until they went to university. They had access to a computer for school projects, learning to type and writing papers. Did they miss out? Absolutely. They missed out on all those hours wasted sitting in front of screens.

Did they feel different from their peers? I hope so. In our house, if they felt different from others, they were on the right track. God created each one of them to be uniquely them—with their own God-given talents and skills. They were not supposed to be like anyone else but themselves. Their job was to figure out what God wanted them to do with their talents.

Did they feel left out of the electronic fun? Perhaps. When they went to friends' houses, they got to enjoy video games and dance pads. Digital technology was and is everywhere, from libraries to orthodontic offices, to museums and restaurants; I saw no reason to fill our space with it. And that is one of the reasons I loved homeschooling. We had control over what was in our environment.

Did they fall behind? Let's see; our eldest is a software engineer who has a full-time job in his field and has done all the programming for a ski resort management tool that he and his cousin invented and marketed. Our eldest daughter is a full-time singer-songwriter, booking agent, and freelance audio engineer. Our youngest daughter can figure out how to use and master any digital device or software. If there is an app or program to aid her university studies, I promise you she has found it, mastered it and shared it with her friends. No. I can vehemently claim that they did not fall behind in this digital age into which they were born. They are all creative, resourceful and motivated individuals with a plethora of skills, talents and interests.

I one hundred per cent believe that the less screen time your children have, the better. The more you read to them and spur the creative juices of the mind, the happier they will be. You will rarely, if ever, have children that complain of boredom. To this day, all of my children's top complaints are that they do not have enough time to pursue their many and varied interests. Reading books is key. Books are big-time boredom busters!

I have heard numerous parents state that they cannot get their children off of their electronic devices. Some of these children are five years old. Others are high school graduates without a job or a desire to pursue higher education. The absolute beauty of homeschooling is that you have complete control over your and your children's environment. What kind of future do you want for your children?

Choose books over movies, television and digital technology intentionally and consistently. If we were starting homeschooling all over again, I would do the exact same thing.

Chapter 2

LEAD BY EXAMPLE

We have all heard the term that the best leaders are those who lead by example.

I remember taking a few courses in marketing at university. One of my professors had first purchased and then built up a huge clientele for a giant grocery chain. I can still remember many of the things he told us because he spoke from experience. He was able to back up what he said with enthusiastic examples and stories.

Another marketing course I took was taught by a professor who had spent years researching entrepreneurs and their marketing practices. Rightly or wrongly, I learned what I needed to pass the course, but very little of it stuck with me. Today, I cannot recall a single thing he taught. I believe it is because he had personally never owned a business.

I believe this is the same with our children. We can tell them something, but if we do not emulate a specific behaviour we deem important, why would they? When they are little, they may obey out of respect, but when they grow up, they are going to make their own choices. I felt that if I was homeschooling them, I needed to lead by example.

Go Outside with Your Children

There is plenty of data to indicate that fresh air, a change of environment and regular movement of our bodies aids in our physical and mental well-being. This applies to both children and adults. When my children were very little, I took them outside every day. I could not just open the door and send them out because they needed my watchful eye to keep them safe. But, I found that many mothers stopped going outside with their children when their children got a little older. I believe this is a gigantic mistake.

When I only had two children, I used to get up before them and go out for a walk or run in the mornings before my husband went to work. When our third, very-busy, never-ending-energy child came along, I relished that extra hour in bed. Who cared about exercise and fresh air when my body craved only sleep? On these days, I took them outside once or twice a day for hours because I knew it was good for them and me. I think I got more exercise keeping my eye on all three of them than I ever did working out for an hour before they woke up in the mornings.

When they got old enough to go out on their own, I rarely if ever stayed inside. I too noticed a huge difference in my mental and physical well-being when I followed my children outside. Realizing that trying to fit in exercise outside of homeschooling was a losing battle, I decided to do whatever they were doing. I believe this is one of the best decisions I ever made.

Now, I am not going to deny that depending on the number of children you have, there are many things that call for a homeschooling mom's attention. Some of these things are correcting lessons, laundry, breakfast, lunch, supper, snacks, calls. The list goes on and on. In my own experience, I found that I had more energy to tackle these items when I regularly went outside every day with my children. And not just for twenty minutes, but for a full hour or two.

If we met to go tobogganing with other homeschoolers, I went up and down that hill with my children instead of freezing at the top of the hill with the other parents. When my children took up skiing, I was right there with them. When I found them second-hand roller blades, I made sure to secure a pair for myself.

I guess my children became so used to me participating that somehow I ended up being the replacement for one of the Venturer scouts that had to cancel last minute for an annual hiking trip to the Adirondacks. As the spot was already paid, they really wanted someone to fill it. At the time, my son was around sixteen years old. He had gone to the final planning meeting for the trip. When he arrived back home, he told me he had great news for me in that I would be able to accompany his company not only as a driver but to participate in the climb as well.

Now, normally, I am game to try anything. But a trip with Kent's Venturer company involved a seven-hour round trip on snowshoes up and down Whiteface Mountain. This mountain is a mere 4867 feet (1483 metres). I really thought some training would have been a grand idea before tackling such a mountain of a project. Well, as my son informed me, the trip was in two days, and he knew I had always wanted to climb a mountain, so he had already told them I would do it.

It was the most physically and mentally challenging endeavour I have ever undertaken. When we made it back to the hotel in time to change and go out to dinner, I clearly remember having to mentally tell my legs to move as I staggered towards the car. The elation I felt from completing the climb and sharing in this amazing experience with my son was so worth it. Inside I felt the proudest that my son had not doubted that I would be able to complete the climb.

Five months later, I found myself cycling along with my son's and daughter's Venturer company as they cycled the 274 km trail that runs tip to tip across the interior of Prince Edward Island. Why would I stay at camp when I could enjoy a spectacular few days enjoying the sun and scenes with this younger crowd? How could I expect my children to grasp the value of getting outside for regular exercise, if I did not?

By going outside every day, I enjoyed the same benefits as my children. They witnessed what a balanced lifestyle looked like, and my husband came home to a motivated, happy, fit family. I do believe that when my children have their own kids, they will remember all the outdoor activities they did with their mom. I truly hope I have passed on the legacy of the importance of enjoying the wonderful world that God created, no matter ones' age.

Unless it was freezing rain, hailing or a thunderstorm, my children went outside every single day for a couple of hours. This occurred from when they were infants to their last year of homeschooling. I accompanied them on ninety-nine per cent of those occasions. If we are trying to teach our children that regular exercise outdoors is important, and we usher them in the backyard without us, what message are we sending them? Is exercise only for children? Is this truly the message we want to deliver?

Get outside every day with your children. The benefits are too great to ignore!

Try Something New

One of the key areas in which I wanted my children to excel was in the ability to manage change successfully. Professionally, this was my area of expertise. I helped organizations and individuals manage significant change. If I could not teach this to my own children, then what business did I have coaching anyone else?

When my daughter took up Karate, I joined along with her. Was I good at it? Absolutely, not. A few of the adults in the class pointed out that it was the first time they had witnessed the Sensei call someone out for using ballet moves. Ha, but no matter, four years into it, and three belts later, I still could not quite get the moves right, but one hundred crunchies twice a week sure did wonders for the core. An added benefit was that when my children were especially ornery, I would stare them down and confidently state, "Watch it, you know I've been taking Karate."

I knew that if I was going to lead by example, it was important that I regularly took up something new—especially something in which I had no prior experience or knowledge. Wanting to demonstrate that true courage meant engaging in things even if one felt scared or uncomfortable, I decided to join a woman's outdoor soccer league. Now I must preface this by stating that I never played any organized sports as a child. In our day, we just went outside and invented things to do. In addition, I had never watched any team sports on television up until this time. I always preferred to be a participant rather than a spectator. I know that sounds unreal, but it is the absolute truth.

So when I took up soccer, I had no knowledge of the sport. Well, when we moved to our new home, in a new neighbourhood, I convinced my neighbour to join the same soccer league I did. She informed me that her husband would be more than willing to provide some coaching from the sidelines as neither of us had played before. This sounded like a great plan.

This was all well and good until three games into the season. I finally managed to dribble the ball with my feet and break away from the crowd. As my friend's husband cheered from the side, a number of my teammates yelled with excitement. With a smile that stretched clear across my face, I aimed at the net. As my foot made contact with the ball, I watched the ball sail towards the net, only to miss by a fraction of an inch. When I turned around and shrugged my shoulders, I realized what all the yelling had been about. I had been going the wrong way. I had nearly put the ball into my own team's net!

Suffice it to say that when my children tried something new and messed up, I shared with them my embarrassing story. When they were frustrated because something was difficult, I could feel their pain and relate appropriately. When they wanted to give up, I encouraged them to give it more time.

Fifteen years later, I still play in that soccer league. More importantly, my three children have repeatedly demonstrated a keen ability to try new things. Whether it is making a cold call regarding a job, moving to a new city completely on their own, inventing and bringing a product to market or making a presentation to a room full of people at work, they all seem to be able to reach beyond their comfort zones, and approach new situations with grit and nervous enthusiasm.

Yes, we have an obligation to our kids to try new things.

Practice Healthy Eating

I think most of us know that whatever we place in our mouths makes a huge impact on our physical well-being. If we regularly stuff in sugar, we feel dopey, droopy and downright lethargic. It steals away our energy like a full day spent in the sweltering sun and humidity. If we want our children at their best to learn, they need a healthy diet. I am not even going to try to explain what that looks like, because there are probably more sites, books and videos dedicated to food and healthy living than any other topic on the internet. You know what I mean by healthy eating.

What I want to highlight is that so often we give the best to our children but fail to give that best to ourselves. Every time we skip lunch or take short cuts with our own eating habits, we not only compromise our health and well-being, but our children once again are watching. Do we want them to learn that healthy eating habits are okay when they are young, but not important if they are a busy mom?

Now, I know this is more of a struggle for some people than others. Much of how we view food and what we consume day to day comes as a direct result of experiences we had growing up. For myself, knowing this motivated me to provide a grand example.

I remember one time someone had purchased a large box of chocolates for me for my birthday. They did this out of love because they knew I loved chocolate. I had opened up the box to share with my children. At one point, my middle daughter reached for a fourth chocolate and bit down on it just as my husband walked in the kitchen and said "Kristy, how many have you eaten?" To which she replied, "four". He looked over at me and asked, "Why aren't you saying something?" to which I replied, "Because I know how she feels."

In the above example, I knew anything I said would not be taken to heart, because my daughter knew how difficult I found it to control my intake of chocolate. But, what she did know was that I never purchased chocolate for myself to bring into the house. It was for special occasions or outings. On my birthday, I would enjoy a piece of chocolate cake with chocolate frosting. Then I would reserve a piece for the following morning for breakfast with a cup of tea. This was repeated for Mother's Day. Outside of that, I did not keep chocolate in the house. I knew I was addicted, and I took measures to combat it.

The mantra in our house was that mom cooked for health, not for taste. I came up with this saying because I wanted my children to understand that healthy food was important, regardless of how it tasted. I cannot think of even one vegetable that my children will not eat today.

LEAD BY EXAMPLE

I am fully aware that our children will make their own choices when they are adults. There is nothing I can do at this point to control or influence whether they decide to make healthy choices or not. But, I can rest in the knowledge that I have done everything in my power to teach them what delineates a healthy food choice by being a living example.

Choose healthy food and feel great, both physically and mentally. Practice what you preach and lead by example in all things.

Chapter 3

SCHEDULE TIME OFF

Now, I believe that parents of homeschooled children probably spend more time with their children than most parents. I am not saying whether this is good or bad—I personally found it to be great—I am just stating it as a fact because the school hours are spent at home. As a result, parenting and homeschooling become a 24 hour, seven days a week occurrence. And because of that, I needed a reprieve. Not an escape when I had escalated to feeling like I was going to burst or keel over from exhaustion, but a regularly scheduled break that ensured I would not get to that extreme.

Schedule a Regular Night Off

In speaking with my homeschooling friends, many of them voiced to me that they felt guilty taking time away from their kids and family. My question was always, "Do you not think that maybe perchance your children might need a break from you?" I know mine did.

It is not always easy to switch off the teaching mode. When my children would say things that were grammatically incorrect, I had to correct them. I just couldn't help myself. When I heard "me and my friends" the little hairs on my neck would rise, and I would say, "my friends and I". My youngest detested these interruptions to her train of thought, saying, "Whatever, Mom, can't you just be a mom right now and not my teacher?" Oh, yes, I believe it is possible that your children need a break, just as much as you do.

So, what to do? Where to go? Depending on your spouse's schedule, or your ability or desire to hire a sitter, the possibilities are endless. The library? I love the library. Go out with friends? Are they available? Take in a movie. It's up to you.

I'll share a few of the things that my friends and I did, and perhaps they will spur a desire in your heart. I encourage you to act on that desire and stick it in your schedule.

If I did not schedule a night out in advance, my reprieve might take me to the grocery store. Sure it made it easier to fly through the aisles or linger at the magazine rack, but it did nothing for my need to feel refreshed. So, I formed the first version of a Tea & Tales group. This name only came to me years later, but it does represent what that very first group entailed.

I sent an e-mail to a handful of homeschooling women, whose company I enjoyed, and invited them for tea, tales and chocolate at the local coffee shop. I left an open invitation, and many of them came every week or two. I, of course, was there every single week, because, as I explained to my husband, I was the organizer, so I had to be there. This always brought a familiar grin to his face as he kissed me on the lips, told me to have a great time and asked me what form of chocolate I would be consuming at the coffee shop, before he closed the door.

Yes, he was on to me. I do so love chocolate. These meetings were such a hit. A handful of us, homeschooling moms, met and we talked about curriculum, children, movies, difficulties and shared ideas. I especially enjoyed those moms who were ahead of me in terms of home-schooling. They became a treasure trove of mentorship for my own homeschooling journey. We laughed, we cried, we sipped tea, and we made sure to order a small snack to stay in the good graces of the coffee shop. Even today, eighteen years later, these women remain my best of friends.

I do admit, I never went home from these evenings until my husband had already settled our children in their beds for the night. One night of freedom per week gave me an edge. I can honestly say I loved homeschooling, and I never became the statistic of someone who homeschooled for three years and gave it up because they were so exhausted and overwhelmed. Yes, I only had three children. No, they did not all magically excel at everything and anything. Homeschooling is hard work. But more importantly, homeschooling is an incredible, fulfilling way of life, and a regularly scheduled break is part of the secret sauce to your homeschooling success. It will prove therapeutic for you, your spouse and your children.

I am so thankful to my husband because he understood this. It may have helped because early on in our homeschooling journey, I showed him a cartoon of a woman. She had wiry hair going in all directions, her clothes were dishevelled with interesting stains on them and her slippers were mismatched. She was holding a baby with a droopy diaper, stirring a pot of liquid mash on the stove while the garbage can overflowed in the background. I told my husband that I loved to homeschool, but that if I did not get a break regularly, I would go psycho. I used the photo to demonstrate what I thought that might look like. He smiled and told me to have a good time each time I walked out the door.

I keep a large calendar posted on our fridge. All events go on that calendar. If my husband forgot to mark in the hockey outing or meeting he set up for that particular night, he would be tasked with finding the babysitter. Anyone flipping through it would see the regularly scheduled meetings booked months in advance.

Schedule a regular night off. Put it in your calendar. Do not cancel, no matter what. You need it!

Choose Sleep Rather Than a Night Out When Necessary

Now, as I am writing this next bit, I know I will have to get permission for this story because this story is not about my family or me, but about a dear friend of mine. It is just too funny not to share, and it fits so well in this part of the book. So, know that I did get permission to tell this story, and no, I am never going to disclose to whom this happened—I already made that mistake once. Obviously, I have changed their names.

Now, for those people who have never had children, you may wonder how what I am about to tell you could ever happen. But, if you are reading this book, I will assume that you have children and you might understand how a lack of sleep, a move to a new city with no friends or family for support, and a baby that is not sleeping through the night, might lead to the situation. I am highlighting this story because sometimes the best time off might mean going into your bedroom and going to sleep, while your husband or babysitter takes over the care of the children.

One of my friends—say her name was Sally—had five children and she was heading out for a bit of a reprieve on her own. My friend's husband—say his name is Jack—changed their baby, put her in a fall jacket and then loaded her into their van. Meanwhile, Sally fetched her purse and the library books she planned to exchange. When Sally exited the house, she stopped first for a quick kiss from her husband and then rounded the front of the van, got up into the driver's seat and was on her way.

As Sally drove along, her littlest one peacefully slept in the car seat behind her. Their destination was only about fifteen minutes away, so they reached the strip mall fairly quickly. Eying a coffee shop at the far end of the mall, my friend exited the van, and headed there for a soothing drink and a small sugary snack. As clichés would have it, she sat and noted the two policemen drinking coffee and eating donuts at the same establishment.

Minutes later, Sally walked past the empty police car and her van, and strode into the library, a mere four doors down from the coffee shop. She made her way around the library, selecting some new books. Then she lined up, waiting to check out her books. As she reached the front counter and was about to hand over her library card, a lady burst into the library and said, "Is there anyone in here with a red van? There's a baby inside that is crying!" All eyes went towards the lady as she continued, "I went to the coffee shop and the two other establishments but couldn't find the owner of the van. The baby is really upset."

Now, I must take a detour with this story, to state straight out that my friend did not intentionally leave her child in the van. This is *not* the funny part.

Sally knew that her husband had put their youngest in the van because he said he would. But since she was the one who usually placed the removable car seat into the van when she went out with her daughter, in her fatigue, she completely forgot her daughter was back there. Coupled with that, her daughter had fallen asleep before she entered the van, so she had not made a sound when they were driving. Add a car seat that must be installed backwards and multiple sleepless nights, and perhaps you can identify with her plight.

When the lady entered the library, looking for the owner of the red van, that is when the light went on in my friend Sally's head. As Sally looked at the librarian's face, she pictured the policemen in the coffee shop. Her saucer-like eyes confirmed that she was now wide awake.

Sally pulled back her hand, which had her library card with her full name on it, just as the librarian was about to take it from her. She thrust the pile of books she had carefully selected on the countertop and abandoned them while saying, "What? Did my husband leave our daughter in the van? Oh my. I can't believe this!" She bolted out of the library, put her key in the lock and drove out of the parking lot in the opposite direction of the coffee shop, with her heart pounding. This is still *not* the funny part.

Sometime after this incident, she shared with me what had happened and the horror she still felt about it. Thankfully everything had turned out fine. Over time, it became one of those horrible experiences she could look back on and be grateful that all had turned out well.

A few years later, Sally and her family moved back into town. One night, my husband and I found ourselves sitting in Sally and Jack's kitchen. For some reason, we were talking about being extremely fatigued. At the time, we were dealing with a sick child who had been in and out of the hospital, and two ailing parents. At some point, I brought up the story of my friend's sleep deprivation and the incident with her daughter.

As my friend is much quieter than I am, she let me tell the story through fits of laughter. Her husband listened intently. Finally, I came to the end of the story and through uncontrollable giggles turned to him and said, "And to think she blamed the whole thing on you, because she was worried about the policemen in the coffee shop who had seen her enjoying her beverage and snack by herself, while your daughter was left alone in the van."

By this time, Sally was biting her lower lip and holding her head in her hand as she turned her body away from the watchful eyes of her husband, Jack. Both Jon and I were beyond control as great streams of tears plunged down our cheeks, and gaggles of sound erupted from our mouths.

Jack's face was not quite so animated as he turned to Sally and asked, "When did this happen?"

I wish I could tell you that our laughter immediately ceased. That would have been the humane thing to do. The truth is that our howls and catcalls got even worse. Through a bumbling mess of giggles and heaving shoulders, I looked at my friend and managed to blurt out, "You never told him?" My eyes darted back and forth between my friend's guilty smile, hidden behind her hand and my friend's husband, who was not laughing at all. I felt it was a perfect time to gather up our children and head home. Thankfully, in the end we all had a good laugh about it—including my friend's husband, Jack.

Yes, you need regular time away from all of your children. Sometimes this might mean going up to your room for some urgent rest while you engage the services of a babysitter, husband or understanding relative or friend. In the early years with our little ones, my husband would get up early on Saturdays and get the children breakfast so I could sleep in, and then in the afternoon, my husband would take a nap while I was on kid duty. This was something we agreed to the night before, so no one's expectations of what "should" happen the next day were out of line.

Sometimes sleep breaks are the best choice for a scheduled time off.

Schedule a Regular Outing With Just Your Spouse.

Your closest confidant can become a stranger if you don't continue to grow as a couple outside of your roles as co-parents. I think most would agree they want their relationship to continue to be as strong or stronger than when they first met. I cannot think of anyone who would disagree that they would love to have a regular outing with their spouse.

The reality of time, finances and finding sitters can deflate this dream in an instant. And that is where I am hoping our experiences of trial and error may be of value to you. At first, we would put aside some time and say, "How about next week we find a night to go to the movies together?" Invariably, due to lack of planning, we would convince ourselves we could just stay in, save some money and just watch a movie together on the television. Yes, this might work once in a while.

In my experience, these nights would be taken over by a child suddenly needing extra care, or someone's favourite pants needing to be laundered, or some essential item requiring a quick trip to the grocery store. If it was not planned, it did not happen. I enjoy spontaneity as well as the next person, but too many times the outing somehow got pushed to the wayside.

One year my husband purchased season tickets to the local live theatre. This provided us with a regularly scheduled outing every six weeks or so over the school year. Oh, how we looked forward to our time together. We usually went for a casual dinner beforehand. Oh, for sure, most of the time we talked about the kids. But as a couple, it kept us scrumptiously close. Yes, I meant to use that word.

The tickets for the theatre were purchased as my Christmas gift. I loved this far more than any trinket or new item for the house. It made us realize the value of the time we spent as a couple. It is probably one of the most memorable Christmas gifts because it told me that my husband wanted to spend time with me.

Babysitting often came from family members, and that was such a huge blessing in our lives. But, we supplemented this with trades with our friends. My husband and I would have our friends' kids over to play for an evening while their parents went out. The following week, we went out while our friends kept our kids. Remember, outings do not have to be in the evenings. A Saturday morning or Sunday afternoon make awesome couple time. Our kids never minded, because they loved to spend quality time with their friends.

Another option is to join a community-run event, such as badminton, volleyball or tennis that runs for several weeks. Once you pay the fee, you are less apt to forgo the outing. I fondly remember our cheap date where we brought roller-blades and skated side by side along the beautiful Rideau Canal in downtown Ottawa. A stop at a local shop for a cool drink rounded out our evening. Another time, for our anniversary, we went to the water park without our kids. The cost was too expensive to justify bringing three kids, six and under, to a water park. An afternoon in the sprinkler would bring the same level of excitement to the wee ones.

SCHEDULE TIME OFF

With our lives now heading towards empty nesters, I am so glad that we took and still regularly book time to spend with each other.

Get out regularly with your spouse. Have fun. Schedule in advance and do not cancel no matter what. Your children will leave one day. I did not want my husband to leave as well.

Chapter 4

STRATEGICALLY PLAN OUT YOUR YEAR

One of the great things about homeschooling is that you have the freedom to design and manage your time. If you want to head out for an early morning physical fitness class with your kids at the local public pool, you can. If you want to avoid the line-up at the hair salon, you can bring your children during a weekday.

This freedom of schedule could be your greatest asset or your worst downfall. Life and managing each day are about prioritizing and reprioritizing multiple life events that come at us from all directions. Illnesses, dental appointments, orthodontic appointments, grocery shopping, a neighbour in need and/or surprise thunderstorm can wipe out carefully made plans in an instant.

We, as well as our children, can use each of these situations as a reason to set school aside for an hour, or a day or multiple days. Pretty soon that grade ten physics book would be looking awfully thick to complete by the end of the school year. Our children and I would soon feel overwhelmed by all that still needed to be accomplished. Next, we would try to squeeze in more and more time for academics, which resulted in a huge imbalance in how our homeschooling days were run. There would be no time left for the "extras" because we had to get done the "absolutes."

Those extras and absolutes are bound to differ between families and children, but when they go haywire, that is when homeschooling loses its luster. I loved homeschooling, and I wanted to keep on loving homeschooling. And now I want to share with you some interesting ways we scheduled our homeschooling year to allow for a positive balance between absolutes and extras.

Do Something Every Day

Each child learns at a different pace. If your child is advancing overall, you are on the right track. I learned early on that if you do a little bit of work every day, your child will progress.

If my children were sick but were well enough to sit up and watch television, they were able to read their current novel for English. Instead of starting the writing assignment associated with it, they might read ahead a few chapters and start the assignment the next day. We rejigged rather than cancelled.

Dental appointments were booked in succession. Math sheets accompanied us to the waiting room. Favourite books were brought for reading after the math sheets were complete.

STRATEGICALLY PLAN OUT YOUR YEAR

Our eldest child was sick on and off for many years. Between the ages of three and a few months short of his twelfth birthday, doctors were unable to diagnose what was ailing him. During this time, he spent eight different times in the hospital that ranged from three to 23 days. Homeschooling assignments kept us all sane. Each day there were long stretches in the hospital between tests and procedures. School assignments, visits to the games and craft room, and medical procedures, filled each day. Having a purpose and moving towards a school goal broke up those difficult times.

Our younger girls often accompanied us to spend the day at the hospital. We would sit in the craft room and work on assignments before delving into the wall of books, games and crafts. My children saw first hand how other children suffered and developed a strong sense of compassion for others. Often they would engage with them in a shared game or craft. If that is not valuable learning time, I do not know what is.

The point I want to stress is that both insignificant and significant things will clamour for your attention. We made a commitment to homeschool and so, like brushing our teeth, we did it every day that we had planned to homeschool. For us, this was Monday to Friday, from September to the end of May. Yes, we took three months off every year. Admittedly, May 31 is my birthday, so perhaps it was a gift to myself. My children certainly did not mind.

Do a little bit every day. Small steps result in huge progress over time.

Divide Your School Year in Half

Each year we—myself, with the input of our children—took the subjects that we deemed were "absolutes" and planned our entire homeschooling year by dividing the material into two equal halves. We scheduled out when, what and how much we were going to cover from September to mid-December. I say mid-December because I always wanted Jesus' birthday celebration to be a joyful celebration, not a stress-filled rush to get everything done. For years we invited other homeschooling friends over to make elaborate gingerbread and crispy rice houses, followed by fort building in the backyard. So we always left plenty of time before Christmas to prepare without having to complete school assignments.

Next, we scheduled out what we would accomplish from January until the end of May. Notice that the second half of our school year was about five months long and the first half of our school year was only about three and a half months. This was deliberate.

When we looked over our year, we tried to divide the total amount of work into two equal parts. For example, if there were ten chapters in science. We would schedule five to be completed before Christmas and five for the remainder of the year. We tried to do this with most of the "absolutes" that we deemed had to be achieved over a year.

The beauty of this approach was multifold. First, my children were always keener and seemed to be able to stay on task at the beginning of the year. When they reached Christmas, they could rest in the knowledge that they had already completed half of their work for the year.

Second, it gave us wiggle room for the second half of the year. In Ottawa, Canada, where we live, January, February and March can be long, cold, snow-packed gloomy months. I have never believed in setting rewards if my children did their work. Instead, I wanted to teach them the value of doing work for its intrinsic value. But, with half of their work completed, I could surprise them with a "you guys have been working really hard, how about we go to a movie theatre this afternoon?" or "How would you like to go visit Grandma directly after lunch." I hope I have been clear on the difference between hanging a carrot in front of them and being able to surprise them with a free day or afternoon in the more challenging months of the year.

Thirdly, we were able to carve out eight to ten successive Mondays during the winter months to go downhill skiing. While others were cooped up in school, we spent the days on the slopes with the seniors and other homeschoolers. A lack of lineups made for a very full day of exercise.

I remember riding the chair lift with a man who told us he was 86 years old. I asked him how he had managed to stay fit enough to tackle the hills. With a glint in his eye, he smiled and said that he just never stopped. Each year, he took out his skis, had them sharpened and waxed and then headed to the hills. It is those moments that I like to think of as homeschooling at its best. What a wonderful life lesson for my children. And who is kidding who, for me as well.

The cost of these outings was incredibly inexpensive. Since the ski resorts were paying for overhead, such as electricity and personnel to run the lifts, they were ecstatic to offer grossly reduced rates to the homeschooling groups who wanted to ski during the weekdays. I think we paid one-quarter of what they charged for a weekend rate. My husband and I surfed the second-hand shops, and never spent more than twenty or thirty dollars, not for each child, but in total—no, I'm not kidding—to outfit our kids with skis and boots from year to year. We traded boots with friends and handed down what fit from child to child. For a number of these years, my husband rearranged his schedule to work Saturdays instead of Mondays so that he could join us on the slopes.

We found winter to be enjoyable because we spent so much time skiing, skating and tobogganing. Our snow-covered property was always filled with snowmen, forts and worn-down trails because we had allocated time in the second half of the year for these types of activities. Winters of homeschooling were celebrated, never dreaded. Oh, the joy that you can enjoy from the flexible nature of home-schooling!

As I mentioned, the second half of the year allowed us to fit in more time for other interests. All three of our children benefitted immensely from this arrangement. Our son, who usually spent numerous hours designing and building everything and anything, received a generous offer from a friend of ours. This man owned a professional training centre that offered courses on AutoCAD, which is a commercial computer-aided design and drafting software application.

This friend of the family recognized our son's interests and invited him to attend a three-hour info session on their course offerings. Then when our son expressed interest, he allowed him to sit at the back of the class with the other participants for a three-day course. Imagine our surprise when he presented our son with an official certificate of completion of the course when he was able to successfully complete all of the tasks along with the other students. These participants already held college degrees. Our son was thirteen years old at the time. Then Kent was invited back for a second three-day course and again was granted a certificate of completion. Yes, time for the "extras", because the "absolutes" were scheduled to be half-finished by Christmas, was a super move!

Our second child, Kristy, was gifted with an incredible voice and ability for piano. She played and sang at Mass for years. At thirteen, she was hired to do all the vocals and piano for a wedding completely on her own, which initiated her music career. From that wedding, someone heard her and booked her for their wedding to be held a few months later. Then someone asked her to play for a funeral. Pretty soon, the local grade school contacted her to play at their grade six graduations. Next, she played at the principals' retreat day. Another year, she and our youngest were given the two main vocal parts for a beautiful fully sung play that highlighted the Christmas story. This was performed at the local school during the day for the entire student population and their parents.

The ironic thing was that our daughter, Kristy, was always homeschooled. She never attended any classes at the local schools. Yet, once someone heard her sing and play, and knew she was available during the day, they had no qualms about booking her for school events.

The funniest time was when Kristy was asked to play at a gathering of school principals. After she played and sang several tunes, the head principal stood up and gave an encouraging talk about how the dedication of each of the principals there that day was a huge contributor to the success of so many children. Then she pointed to Kristy and stated that she was the result of what great schools, teachers and principals' produce. Obviously, the person who had booked Kristy had not informed this particular principal that Kristy was homeschooled and was not a product of their institution. We did not feel the need to enlighten her, but we sure had a chuckle about it on the way home.

One year, we purchased a sewing machine for our youngest daughter, Brooke, as her main Christmas gift. Next thing we knew, a wonderful lady from our church offered to teach her how to sew. Over a year and a half, Brooke spent numerous half days with this lovely lady, who told us none of her grandchildren had any interest in learning the craft. Often, Brooke would phone prior to me picking her up, insisting that she and Jackie wanted to continue for a few more hours as they both loved to talk and sew. A wonderful friendship developed between a seventy-five-year-old grandmother and a fifteen-year-old homeschooler. Since this time, Brooke has completed many beautiful projects for both family and friends. The flexibility of home-schooling and a wonderful kind-hearted lady afforded her this opportunity.

Strategically plan out your homeschooling year, so you have time to incorporate special activities and opportunities. These may turn out to be some of your children's most valuable teaching moments!

Practice Mastery Before Moving On

I have been asked the following question so many times I decided to include it here. Many parents have wondered if my children had trouble retaining the mathematics they had learned from the previous year. My answer is not really, even though we took a three-month break from homeschooling each summer. Our experience demonstrates that it has much more to do with mastering a subject before moving on.

For any of the sciences, if my children did not attain 85% on a test, we went back and reviewed the sections with which they had issues. It was never a problem; it just meant we needed to go back and spend some time on the parts they misunderstood. We would never move on until we did this together or as a teen, they went back and reviewed these sections themselves, and I stepped in when they could not quite figure it out. So in effect, they were required to master a subject before they moved forward. Sometimes a particular area took more time and other times they would be able to whip through certain sections. It all kind of evened itself out.

Mastery is key to the learning of mathematics. If this does not happen at each step, it is highly likely your child will come to detest math. Now I should mention here that I studied pure mathematics up to second year in university, before switching faculties. I originally chose math because I had no idea what I wanted to do, and it was always my easiest subject. So I understand the foundational nature of the study of mathematics.

I truly believe that there are two significant reasons people have trouble in math. The first is because they are forced to move on regardless of whether or not they have fully grasped the concept under study. Because math builds upon itself, mastery of each concept is essential. When this does not take place, a person's ability to understand more complex concepts will crumble. In school, teachers must keep moving forward to cover the material for a particular grade. You do not have to do this with homeschooling!

If your child is having trouble with addition, do not go to subtraction. Children develop at different rates. One child may be musically inclined, while another is verbally inclined, while the third is mathematically inclined. They can all learn math; they just may not progress at a predefined pace. If you insist they move on without full understanding, they will become frustrated, and you will become stressed. This is not an ideal learning environment. Work hard at it every day, and over time, they will progress. If you have to spend a month on one topic, so be it. Do not be a slave to your curriculum.

The second reason people have trouble learning math is that it is not taught logically. Topics are presented in a random or haphazard fashion. This is not the fault of teachers; often, it is the fault of whoever wrote the curriculum teachers are required to use. This can be further compounded by students who move from a different province or state, move to a different school where the math curriculum for a particular grade varies from their old school. Homeschooling allows a consistent curriculum in a subject that requires a step-by-step approach.

I promised myself I would not get into curriculums in this book because there are so many variables when choosing a curriculum that suits your child. But, suffice it to say, I am extremely opinionated on mathematics' curriculums. We found a video-based one, and before we purchased it, I borrowed the videos from a friend. I may be crazy, but I spent a weekend and completely watched eleven grades of math instruction. I needed to see the succession of how and when the material was presented. I knew when I bought Math-U-See, all three of my children would come to excel at math. It did not disappoint. Ah, but I digress and broke my promise. Some things are too important not to share!

Getting back to how we ensured our children retained what they learned from the previous year, we repeated a particular practice each September. I would either save a cumulative math test from the previous year, or I would photocopy it before they completed it at the end of the year and re-administer it during their first week back to school in September. This test never counted towards a mark.

The purpose was for them to simply take the test to jog their memory. If they had trouble or got stuck at any of the questions, they were allowed to go back to their textbook and look up how to solve those particular types of problems.

The point I am trying to relay is that because my children were used to mastery before moving on, they rarely had trouble working through the math test from the previous year. It can be likened to riding a bicycle, once you learn how to do it or master it, it takes very little effort to pick it up again. But, if you never spent enough time to learn how to balance on a bike one year, it would be like you were starting from scratch the next year. Thus, working through the test each September was no big deal. It just reminded them of what they had mastered the year before.

This notion of mastering a subject before moving on can be applied to all aspects of homeschooling. Some children learn to read at four years of age while others master it at seven, eight or nine years old. If they are forced to handle material because it is a certain grade level, but they are not ready for the material, you are only going to cause frustration for you and your child. Besides you risk taking away a love of learning from children who are naturally curious. Alternatively, if your six-year-old can read at a grade six level—yes, this did happen to our middle child— continue to challenge them with resources at that higher level rather than holding them back because they are still working in a lower grade in other subjects. The beauty of homeschooling becomes so apparent when we are not worried about what grade levels our children are supposed to be at but rather that we can guide our children at a pace that is suited to their unique skills and talents in the various subjects.

Practice mastery before moving on. This will set up your children for success.

Chapter 5

STRENGTHEN YOUR SUPPORT SYSTEM

As much as I believed in homeschooling, there were times when I would wonder if it was worth it. Theoretically, it all sounded great. But when no one seemed to be listening, or the writing assignment loomed, or I had no idea what we would be having for dinner, and the laundry bucket was so putrid you could smell it from across the house, I have to admit that the thought did cross my mind that perhaps I was crazy for taking on homeschooling.

As I passed the bathroom, the vision of myself buried under large bubbles enjoying a hot soak with my nose buried in a novel beneath low lit lighting came to mind. Sometimes I would enter the kitchen, open the dishwasher and discover that I had forgotten to turn it on. While stashing more lunch dishes into the sink, my mind would suddenly flash to an image of my body lying in a hammock. There I was swinging slowly as warm sun rays kissed my cheeks, the sound of chickadees danced in my ears and the sweet aroma of new spring flowers tickled my nose. Imagine if my children were at school right now, whatever could I be doing?

So yes, sometimes I wondered if it was worth it. These were the precise times when I had to rely on my support system to get me over the hump and back into the fun of home-schooling. There are a number of elements that you need to have in place to ensure this happens.

Research Data on Homeschooling

In cases when I was not feeling up to the task of home-schooling, I would turn to homeschool facts to carry me over those mental roadblocks. When we started home-schooling, there were only a few long-term studies that touted the success rate of homeschoolers. But even then, I held onto the data and kept these reports close at hand. A quick glance over the success of homeschoolers always gave me a burst of mental energy to move forward.

There are many reasons why you may have chosen home-schooling for your children. So I would not want to presume they are the same reasons why our family decided to homeschool. Instead, I would suggest you search online for data on any of the following questions or others that are important to you:

What percentage of homeschoolers go to college? How well do homeschooled kids fare at college or university?

Do homeschoolers get good jobs?

The information on homeschooling success is so prevalent now. Find the reasons that spurred you to homeschool in the first place. For our family, it was the flexible lifestyle, the superior academic success of homeschoolers as a whole, and the track record of homeschoolers being accepted and faring well in colleges and universities.

Did any of these facts guarantee the individual success of my children? No. But did the overwhelming track record of previously homeschooled versus traditionally schooled individuals motivate me to continue homeschooling? Absolutely.

Find the data on homeschooling that speaks to you. Summarize it in a one-page document. Post it somewhere you will see it (e.g. your fridge or mirror). Refer to it often.

Be Proactive and Educate Your Family and Friends

When we decided to homeschool, I had a conversation with each of my four siblings, my parents, my in-laws and my close friends, on our decision. I did not ask for any of their opinions. As none of them had homeschooled or researched homeschooling, I knew their opinion did not carry any weight. Instead, I shared with them our intention and the list of reasons why we had decided to try homeschooling for a year.

When our family and friends asked all of the typical questions regarding socialization, legalities of home-schooling, how will they be tested, did I not need to be a teacher, etc. I knew the answers because I had researched them ahead of time. I made sure to answer their questions with a "That's a great question, I wondered the same thing at first and here is what I discovered…", or if I didn't know the answer, I would respond with, "Wow, great question, I had not considered that. Thank you, I'm certainly going to look into it." Of course, I did follow-up and investigate. I felt it was my job to equip myself with the answers.

With this approach, I was able to educate my sphere of influence. Most told me that it was not something they could see for their own family, but they respected our family's decision to homeschool.

One of my sisters told me a few years later that when we first informed her that we had decided to homeschool, she initially thought we were crazy. She never mentioned it at the time because I seemed to be knowledgeable about it. After a while, she told me that she had felt we had made a good decision for our family. She admitted she had never heard of homeschooling prior to our initial conversation and was bewildered as to why we would choose something so out of the ordinary.

Most of my family and friends shared that they had either never heard of homeschooling or they never actually met anyone that homeschooled. I loved to watch their eyes widen when I told them that I belonged to a home-schooling organization that had hundreds of registered families, who met regularly for support and shared activities. Today, you would be hard-pressed to find someone who has not heard of homeschooling. But their perceptions of homeschooling may not match the reality. I felt it was my duty to educate my family and friends on homeschooling by proactively having a conversation with them when we first started and enthusiastically answering their questions as time went on.

Notice that earlier, I mentioned that I told people we were going to try homeschooling for a year. I highly encourage you to take it a year at a time. Each family is different, and each situation is different. There are probably as many reasons to put a child in school as there are to homeschool. So, the wonderful thing about homeschooling is that you have the freedom to choose.

In our case, the advantages always outweighed the disadvantages of homeschooling. This was true for each and every year we decided to homeschool. Do not overwhelm yourself wondering if you have the stamina to homeschool for the next five, ten or eighteen years. Take it a year at a time and evaluate year to year, based on your goals and ideals for your unique family and situation.

Educate your family and friends on why you have chosen to homeschool. Re-evaluate your choice every year.

Increase the Support of Your Spouse

I have met many families that homeschool. In many cases, the parent who is not doing the homeschooling is a huge support to the homeschooling process. This is ideal. But, I have witnessed enough times where the spouse was either negative or neutral.

I do not purport to say that I can help you change your spouses' mind about homeschooling; that is really his (or hers, if the primary homeschooler is the father) decision to make. But, I am definitely going to claim that he needs a certain level of proof that homeschooling is the way to go.

Challenges of homeschooling can come in many forms. Perhaps your children are unmotivated, you feel overwhelmed, and your friends and family are unsupportive to name a few. If your husband is not fully on board, you might feel you are climbing an uphill battle all on your own.

I have heard homeschoolers say that their spouses were neutral about homeschooling. They were told that if they wanted to homeschool that was perfectly fine with them. But, these were the same women who gave up homeschooling because they were not getting any support from their spouse. When they were having difficulties, their spouse would merely encourage them to put the kids in school and be done with it.

In our case, I was working as a professional in a high-tech firm up until the due date of our first child. I resigned to be home full time with him. As our next two children came along, I continued to stay at home. My plan had always been to return to full-time work once our youngest entered school.

When we started to homeschool, I had a five-year-old, a three-year-old and a newborn. At first, we were just going to try it for a year. But, at the end of a year, we loved it so much, we tried it another year. As time went on, it became clear that homeschooling was a great fit for our family. But this decision came with huge financial ramifications. On those difficult days or weeks of homeschooling, it was important to me that my husband was consistently in support of our decision.

I first heard about homeschooling when our eldest child was only three years old. At the invitation of an acquaintance, I decided to attend a live homeschooling conference in my area. I was enthralled with both the idea and the caliber of people that I met. The next year, I asked my husband to accompany me to the conference. He shared my excitement because he met families that were actually homeschooling and were excited and knowledgeable. Afterwards, we discussed the pros and cons, and made a decision together.

As new studies came to light, I continued to share this information with my husband. At the end of each homeschooling year, we sat together and talked about the year, what gains each of our children had made individually, and then how our family had grown collectively in the values and beliefs that we held dear. It always seemed to come back to the fact that our children were progressing and that our family was really close. Neither of us saw any reason to jeopardize what was working well.

Regardless of who is the primary homeschooler in your family, both parents glean massive value from attending a homeschooling conference together. Seeing is believing!

Do Not Allow Negative Family or Friends to Discourage You

I remember this one particular relative; she thought it was her duty to voice her concerns regarding our choice to homeschool our children. This particular relative was quite a bit older and had never heard of homeschooling. Out of love and concern for our children, she felt compelled to strongly advocate for her belief that our children should be in school. On many occasions, she would pointedly ask direct questions implying that our children needed to be in school. I could have let this bother me and fester with each visit. Instead, I decided to use it to our advantage.

Whenever we would visit, I would have the children bring something on which they had worked and of which they were particularly proud. This could be a story they wrote, a model of something they had built or a new piece of music they had learned to play. This enhanced the relationship between my children and this relative because it gave her a glimpse into the things on which they had worked. She felt honoured that they wanted to share with her what they were learning. In turn, my children felt validated that what they had spent time working on was interesting and worthwhile to someone outside our immediate family.

I cannot say that the questioning ever went away with this relative. I think she felt strongly that it was her duty to express her view on homeschooling. But, I do know that over time, she would comment on how intelligent the kids were nowadays with all the things they knew. Eventually, more and more of her questions turned to precise enquiries into what they were currently studying. Each of my children came to enjoy these precious visits, and I believe it was mutual.

Find creative ways to highlight your children's successes with close relatives; it will benefit everyone.

Do Not Share Negative Instances With Negative People

I truly hope that your extended family is excited or at least respectful of your decision to homeschool. But I know that this is not always the case. This can lead to feelings of stress and resentment when you are obligated to be in the presence of these individuals due to a family event or gathering. But there are a few ways that you can minimize this negativity.

Do not share your challenges or frustrations about homeschooling with individuals you already know are negative about homeschooling. Now, as I mention this, I think it sounds so obvious. So I think it is best to provide an example to illustrate precisely what I mean.

Imagine yourself lingering over coffee and dessert at the close of Thanksgiving dinner. The children are in another room watching a movie, and the person to your right has always been negative or unsupportive about your homeschooling. Imagine next that your mother across the table asks you how Kent is doing with his writing. For years, this has been a difficult skill for your son to master. Your mother is asking out of interest. In this situation, my first instinct was to share the truth of how frustrating the progress was and how concerned I was that Kent might never master writing.

Then remember who is sitting beside you—the person who is negative about homeschooling. On every occasion that I brought up any challenges, the persistently negative person seemed to feel this was an opportune time to advocate why this child should be placed in real or regular school.

Sometimes they may feel this is an opportune time to convince others of this as well. I recall mentally kicking myself when I realized how I had once again fallen into this trap. We all know, for some people, that nothing we say is going to change the other person's mind about homeschooling.

When I spoke with some of my homeschooling friends, a number of them shared that they got caught in the same trap—often with family members. Finally, I decided that this would not happen again, and realized that the last thing I would do would be to complain or voice my frustration. Instead, I would say, "Kent and I are working very hard on it" and then I would steer the conversation to another area in which he was excelling. At a separate time and place, I would converse openly with the other family member who was genuinely interested in how things were going, and were ready to offer support and understanding.

Do not share your frustrations with people that are consistently negative about homeschooling.

Reduce Time Spent With Negative People

One of the areas on which I have counselled my children is being mindful of with whom they spend their time. When they were young, if a child in the playground kept throwing sand and my children started to do the same, I would remove them from the situation. As they became teenagers, I would tell them that if they are hanging around someone whom they know is influencing them to make bad decisions, then they needed to reduce the amount of time they spent with this person. Sometimes that meant spending little or no time with them at all. We owe it to our families and to ourselves to do the same.

If there are individuals who continue to berate your homeschooling choice, you need to reduce or eliminate the time you spend with them.

Find a Homeschooling Mentor

I want to give credit here to my homeschooling mentor, a wonderful lady by the name of Betty. Her youngest was the same age as my eldest. We each had three children, but she was about six years ahead of me in terms of homeschooling. She knew what it was like to homeschool a pre-teen or teenager long before I did because she had been through it. When I reached that point, she was always a welcome resource.

I met Betty through various homeschooling activities, and we attended the same Bible study group for years. About twice a year, I made a point of contacting her to go for dinner so we could talk about our children. Here I tried to glean everything I could about her homeschooling journey. What worked, what did not, how to tweak things for different personality types or learning styles. I was quite open with her that I considered her my mentor, and she was always gracious enough to agree to a night out for dinner. I cannot tell you how many times she said something or shared a situation that fit with exactly what I needed to hear at that particular point in time. I am so thankful for her willingness to share her wisdom with me for all of those years.

Find someone a few years ahead of you and glean their wisdom over a shared meal.

Meet With Other Homeschoolers

A few years into homeschooling, I decided that I was not going to attend the annual homeschooling conference because it clashed with another commitment. In my mind, I justified it because I had been homeschooling for a while and felt that things were going relatively well so the conference was not that important. At the last minute, things got rearranged and I was able to go. I must say, was I ever glad I did!

I remember driving home from the conference thinking about everything I would have missed if I had not been in attendance. I always learned something new from the speakers that fit with things with which my children or I were struggling. I was able to pick up some resources for the upcoming year and save on shipping costs. Most of all, it placed me in a room with hundreds of engaged and positive homeschoolers.

The conference reminded me in a very tangible way that my family was not alone in this journey, that homeschooling was an amazing way of life and that the women who homeschooled were women of character that I wanted to emulate. It confirmed to me, year after year, that we were on the right track, and when we were not, it gave me the tools and knowhow to point us back in the right direction.

Go to a homeschooling conference in your area. Make it a priority regardless of how long you have been home-schooling.

Join Some Homeschooling Groups

Today, there are many homeschooling blogs, videos and groups that you can access in an instant online. Certainly take time to check some of these out and select one or two that you find are uplifting. The only caution I have is to be conscious of how much time you are spending online. In my experience, it is much more pleasing to meet with other homeschoolers over coffee or a shared event than spending hours online.

In Ottawa, I had the opportunity to tie into a home-schooling association that held monthly meetings in the evenings. Each meeting had a guest speaker, a second-hand curriculum table and some coffee/tea and snacks. I rarely missed a meeting as I scheduled these into my calendar and made them a priority. Each time I went, I met more homeschoolers and gained new ideas on how to improve our homeschooling experience. It was a night out that I always thoroughly enjoyed.

The more I engaged with other homeschoolers, the better our homeschooling became. There was nothing like having a constant line into a group of like-minded educators. I listened, learned, and sought help for the particularly difficult aspects of the homeschooling lifestyle. Here was a safe place to voice my concerns or challenges and seek solutions from those who had gone ahead.

Join a homeschooling group.

Chapter 6

SEEK VOLUNTEER OPPORTUNITIES

I am not sure where you currently reside, but in Ontario, Canada, the schools instituted a requirement that high school students must complete forty hours of volunteering to graduate from high school. These hours are to be completed anytime from grade nine to grade twelve. The reality that schools had to institute this requirement floored me. Yet, I heard time and again of teens trying to squeeze in their forty hours at the last minute so they could graduate. How difficult is it to volunteer a mere ten hours per year of one's time?

Throughout four summers, I was responsible for hiring staff for a local charity that provided vacations for families in need. We usually received a stack of applicants from students looking for summer positions. I can tell you with all sincerity that one of the main things I was looking for was whether the applicant had volunteered in some capacity in their community.

I remember receiving a resume of a girl whose marks were top notch. She had participated in many sports and excelled at all of them. Her cover letter and resume had been created with much detail and care. She came to her interview sharply dressed and looked me in the eye when she shook

67

my hand. I knew upon meeting her that she should be able to perform any of the duties at the charity for which she had applied. The interview went fine as she clearly articulated her responses to the interview questions. I did not hire her.

In all of her experiences, she had worked hard, but she had never in any capacity volunteered for anything. Everything she had done was directly or indirectly for her benefit. Here, we were running a camp for families in need for eight successive weeks where families were on-site twenty-four hours a day, seven days a week. As soon as these families stepped on the property, we wanted them to feel welcomed, loved and appreciated. Perhaps this was judgemental, but I could not ascertain whether this beautiful girl would know what it meant to truly give of herself to these families.

Yes, I decided after a mere thirty-minute interview that she would not get one of the jobs. But the staff we did hire were able to share with me how they had given to their community. You could see it in their eyes when they spoke from the heart, and relayed situations when they gave of their time and talents with no expectation of anything in return. They gave of themselves because of the intrinsic value of doing so, not because they had a forty-hour quota to meet. Everyone we hired had hundreds of volunteer hours. They did not disappoint.

I feel privileged to have had the opportunity to mentor youth exuding with compassion and love for others. I wanted to foster these traits in my children. Volunteering affords that.

Volunteering Fosters Accountability

When my children were between the ages of twelve and fourteen years old, I noticed that their drive to complete schoolwork suddenly went down. Where they were motivated in the past, they suddenly felt the futility of what they were doing. This was when I discovered that they needed to be accountable to someone other than myself. Herein lay a key value of volunteering.

If they said they had to be somewhere, they kept their promise. I remember my daughter missing a birthday party because she had already agreed to help out at our church. Without asking me, she went ahead and told her friend that she appreciated the invite, but that she would not be able to attend because she had a prior commitment. Now, this daughter loved parties, and many of her close friends were going to be there.

When she shared this with me, I explained to her that with enough notice, they could perhaps make other arrangements at our church. She responded with, "Mom, I know they don't have anyone else to fill in, so I made a commitment, and I am going to keep it." This daughter is now in her twenties, and she is known for her accountability. When she says she is going to do something, she does it. She is a person of her word.

Character traits of being responsible and accountable can be fostered via volunteering.

Keep It Simple

I believe there comes a time in all of our lives when we need help from another person. Whether it be someone to watch our children during an emergency, financial difficulty or we age and are bedridden. Imagine if no one ever took notice of us in our times of need. What kind of world would that be?

I wanted my children to realize that giving of themselves is a normal and natural part of life. So, they began volunteering at a very young age. One of the things we were involved in was designing a simple craft each week for twenty-two pre-school children whose moms were at the same Bible study group I attended. We did this for three school years, which meant we needed to shop for, cut out pieces and come up with forty unique crafts each year.

At the time, my children were three, six and eight years old. While the two eldest focused on generating ideas and gathering items, my youngest was responsible for assembling the items to make a sample for the kids to follow. Once at Bible study, our two oldest would aid the pre-schooler teacher with craft set up, assembly and takedown. Our littlest one loved to walk up to the moms and point out that she had helped design the craft that their particular child was holding. She had not learned humility yet, but she, at three years old, experienced the thrill of serving another person.

When we moved to a new neighbourhood, we discovered that our next-door neighbour, Rolex, was on long-term disability due to an accident while his wife still worked full time. He spent many days alone at home or puttering in his garden. This provided an ideal arena for our children to serve. When we went strawberry or apple picking, our children would come home and help wash up the fruit before delivering a care package to the neighbour. He was thrilled. Next, they baked muffins or cupcakes, and my youngest, Brooke, was always the first one to suggest that they needed to wrap some up for Mr. Rolex. Next, the kids would be brainstorming what else they could do to surprise him.

It always made Mr. Rolex laugh when he would be walking between our houses or working in his backyard, and suddenly he would hear Brooke bellow from the inside of the screened window, "Hi, Mr. Rolex. What 'cha doing?" It did not matter if it was summer or winter; Brooke would slide the window wide open, so she did not miss a chance to engage in conversation. I have to admit that I was not always impressed when I discovered she had neglected to close the window afterwards! But, I did love how much she reached out to engage with our neighbour.

I recall a time when our son was eleven years old. We were sitting in church listening to a couple speak about their missionary work in one of the poorest parts of India. The presenters had both been teachers, but as part of their retirement had decided to open a school for these youngsters in India. The couple had a collage of photos, one of which was of some children holding large green leaves with mounds of white rice sitting in the middle of them. The couple went on to explain how most of the families were unable to provide lunch for their children. So the school would cook rice every day, and the kids were tasked with collecting large leaves as bowls for their noon meal. The couple closed the presentation by asking people to donate funds for the school.

My son turned to me and asked if he could give the birthday money he received to the couple's school mission. Allowance was not something we ever gave our children. Any money they had was either earned through a job or given to them at Christmas or their birthdays by relatives. At the time, our son had one hundred dollars to his name. He did not have any other savings.

I explained to him that he could certainly take some of his money to donate. He asked if it was okay if he gave all of his money. I shared with him that it was not necessary to give all of his money away, but that a percentage of maybe ten or fifteen per cent would suffice. At this, he turned to me and said, "Mom, I have everything I could ever need, want or desire, so why can't I donate all of my money?" With tears in my eyes, I nodded my agreement. At eleven years old, he truly understood what it meant to fully give to others. The last thing I wanted to do was to rob him of this opportunity.

Simple acts of volunteering nurture the importance of giving to others.

Volunteer as a Family

When our family moved on-site to serve at a charity for three-and-a-half years, this was not a paid position for any of us. From the day we moved into the farm-like setting, our children had chores above and beyond their regular household responsibilities. Whether it was mucking the barn, feeding the chickens, running the bingo, cleaning cottages, preparing crafts or finding wood for the bonfire they were actively engaged with us.

As my husband held a full-time job during the day, and I had a part-time consulting job, while homeschooling and running the charity with two other families, our children saw their mom and dad serve others despite our fatigue. This cannot be taught. I believe it must be witnessed. Some of our family's fondest memories are of this time we spent at the farm.

Our youngest is now in university and volunteers with three different organizations. I love when she sends a photo of herself dressed in a bear's costume, entertaining the kids of parents who are donating blood or when she tells me about the training she attends every two weeks with a search and rescue organization in Newfoundland. Last week, she laughed as she told me she "somehow now helps out with the young children's program at her church." I love to hear her speak with excitement about all she is doing while managing her course load and working to pay for her schooling. I feel the joy in her heart!

Whether it is at your church, a soup kitchen, a senior's residence, or for a neighbour, find a way to volunteer with your children. There is no greater feeling than serving another—what a wonderful gift to give to your children and society.

Chapter 7

START OR JOIN A HOMESCHOOLING CO-OP

A homeschooling cooperative occurs when homeschooled children get together with other homeschooled children for shared activities. The term cooperative implies that the homeschooling parent is present and participates in the shared activities. This can take many forms.

In our experience, over the eighteen years of homeschooling, we were involved in many different forms of cooperatives. Each has its advantages, but I must say it is difficult for me to think of many disadvantages of these cooperatives. My children and I loved them so much that we often still talk about these times and all the amazing things we did together. I will describe each of them in turn. Hopefully, some of these will resonate with you.

Six-Year-Old Club

When my eldest was six years old, and we were into the second year of homeschooling, we started a group called the Six-Year-Old Club. It was held for two hours every

Friday in one of four homes. As I had a four-year-old and a very busy one-year-old, I welcomed the chance for my son to get together weekly with three other children his age. The best part was that the four mothers alternated turns for hosting the event. In effect, each of us ran the cooperative in our own home every fourth week.

In this type of co-op, I would drop off Kent at one of the houses on Fridays afternoons and leave for the two hours. So I was a participant only one of the four weeks. Each Mom decided what activity they would do with the children.

Our family loved science, so we usually did something to do with magnets or electronic kits. One mom loved to bake, so she would help the kids make cookies or build structures out of marshmallows and toothpicks. Another mom, who had five older children, sometimes had her other children run the group by playing board games or arranging obstacles courses in the backyard. The fourth mom loved to do crafts with the children.

The next year the group became the Seven-Year-Old Club. In each case, since we all had other children, when the club was held at our house, those children could attend as well. Overall, we liked it because two hours seemed to be a perfect length of time for the age of the kids, it provided a change of environment for the children in the club, and it allowed me to have some one-on-one time with just our four-year-old while our baby, Brooke, had her afternoon nap.

This type of co-op works best when the participants live geographically close together.

Friday Co-op

My family's memories of this group are especially fond as some of their first friends were made as a result of participating in this type of group setting; many of them are still friends today. Although they do not currently reside in the same city; they will still touch base from time to time via Skype or when they are back in the city for a visit with family.

This co-op took place every second Friday afternoon from September to May. At the beginning of the year, each mom put forth ideas for possible outings. These included things such as festivals, museums, hiking, tobogganing, bowling, swimming, skating and painting. There was a huge focus on outdoor activities, and the variety appealed to the children. We scheduled the whole year and had the awesome resource of a local church hall that we could use as a back-up when the weather did not fit with our plans.

Activities were either no cost or low cost. The nice thing was you were not obligated to attend any of the events. People were asked to inform the group two days prior, so everyone knew how many people to expect. No money exchanged hands between homeschoolers as each family paid the establishments directly.

This co-op ran for several years. I believe the success was due to the yearly planning and the ability to attend or not. There was definitely a core of homeschoolers that only missed when a child was ill. Our family always looked forward to these events and made our Friday mornings run smoother as everyone looked forward to the outings.

One activity involved taking canvases, paint and paintbrushes to the annual Tulip Festival in Ottawa. The children and adults would spread out on the grass, and capture the beautiful images of the multi-coloured tulips that adorned the pathways next to the Rideau Canal, which boasts being the longest skating rink in the world during the winter months. The greatest pleasure came from the tourists who would walk by and ooh and ahh at the children's canvases while asking to take photos of their work. These are the experiences that occupy my mind whenever I think back to our wonderful years of homeschooling. I would not trade those days for anything!

This co-op has the potential for children to build lasting friendships with other homeschooled children.

Multi-age Enrichment Co-op

This next type of co-op is best when you have multiple children. This one was a huge hit with our family as we participated for eight or nine years. This enrichment co-op had already been running a few years before we started homeschooling so by the time we joined, it was a well-oiled machine.

The main structure of this type of co-op is that it ran for eight weeks in the fall and eight weeks in the winter. This gave families a month to settle back into homeschooling each September, allow a sufficient break for Christmas, and avoid some of the nasty winter driving we are faced with every year in Ottawa. As this co-op required some preparation time on the part of the mothers, it was essential that it did not run all year long.

Each Thursday afternoon, throughout the eight-week session, all of the families involved would gather for a 15-minute session to reconnect, hear announcements and sing our national anthem together. Then we would split the children into five different age groups, including a nursery and a teen group at the older end. Each child would attend three 45-minute sessions taught by the moms involved in the co-op.

Each September, the moms were asked to provide an outline of several course ideas that they would be comfortable teaching, the corresponding age groups for which they were intended, and the estimated costs of supplies per student for materials. The idea was to provide one physical fitness, one art and one other type of class, for each of the age groups. This would enable homeschooled children to participate in activities that often worked better in a group setting. For example, one of the offerings of a particular age group might be soccer, drama and public speaking.

Now the great thing about this type of co-op is that homeschooling moms come from so many varied backgrounds that together the multitude of course offerings was astounding. I loved it when I became the co-director and had a hand in choosing and scheduling the courses. It was so exciting to see the offerings come together for each of the age groups. The students were usually as excited as the teachers.

Now, for this to be a pleasant experience, each mom only had to prepare for one class that would run the full eight weeks. So each week she came to the co-op, she would teach for one 45-minute session, help out for one 45-minute session and then be on break for one 45-minute session.

The beauty of this arrangement is that even a mom with multiple children would get a 45-minute break when she could converse with other homeschooling moms also on their break. I can tell you from experience that these moms relished this time. Many stated it was the highlight of their week, and often the only outing they had from week to week. Of course, we always made sure that there was a nice snack, as well as hot chocolate, assorted teas and coffee to heighten the experience.

One year that I ran this co-op, we had 17 families and 54 children involved. It ran just as smoothly as when we had half that number. I think this is in part due to a few of the rules that we instituted early on. If a family member was ill and could not attend, the entire family did not attend that week. The mom that usually helped in that class was responsible for running the class of the absent mom for that week. This may sound harsh, but after trial and error, everyone agreed that this worked best. It avoided people dropping off their kids and expecting those at the co-op to supervise them. If you had two families do this who had multiple children, it tended to be too chaotic.

A second rule was that there was to be no assigned homework from the classes. This way, it would not interfere with the varied schedules of the homeschooled children. Most of the kids involved never thought of the co-op as being a part of their schooling.

Another thing we strongly recommended was that the moms teaching keep things simple so that they did not have to bring too many supplies or spend a great deal of time preparing. For example, leading a class of 4-6-year-olds might involve setting up a series of stations, such as a Lego table, a large piece puzzle, some magnetic letters and small whiteboards. One of the moms did this and just switched out week to week from what was on her shelves from home. At the end of her 45 minutes, she had the children play a game that involved picking everything up. Smart!

I did much of my preparations for the year during a day or two in the summer. I especially enjoy teaching teenagers. As I come from a corporate business background, I loved to teach things like public speaking, critical thinking, creative thinking and time management through interactive games and exercises. Preparation was quick because these are things I knew inside and out, and therefore, I could pretty much facilitate a class from a basic outline. Additionally, I am a huge proponent of exercise, so I often took on one of the outdoor education classes. Other than remembering to bring assorted balls and some pylons, I did not need to do much preparation. The teens always had great suggestions for new games and were more than willing to take the lead in physical fitness areas where I had limited knowledge.

One semester, one of the moms decided to teach Civics. Before I knew it, she had set up a series of classes leading to a full election. The kids chose political candidates, developed platforms, made speeches and put up posters.

The buzz of excitement that went on amongst the students as election day approached was like watching kids at Disneyland.

On election day, the male candidate showed up in a full suit, his shoes shining and his hair coiffed. At first, I did not even recognize him. He had taken the class very seriously. The entire co-op was given a chance to approach a real polling station to cast their vote. It was incredible! This talented mom had found a way to involve every child, and draw out their individual strengths and talents. The learning that went on in such a fun, engaging, positive atmosphere was amazing!

Other examples of courses we ran were: cooking, science experiments, badminton, track and field, drama, painting, drawing, calligraphy, crafts, scrapbooking, and Canadian history.

The cost of this co-op was so reasonable. We charged $50 per family for the two eight-week sessions. Each child was given an outline with the supplies they needed to bring to each class; simple things like pens, pencils, paper, duo-tangs. The fees we collected were re-distributed to any of the classes that required special items (such as food for cooking classes or photocopies). We held this co-op at a wonderful church where we were able to give a monetary amount to help cover heat, hydro, and bathroom supplies.

I cannot say enough about this type of co-op experience. Although the co-op was structured, its primary purpose was to give our children a chance to interact with other homeschoolers, and the moms an opportunity to network and build friendships. Even when my eldest started some university classes part-time, he tried to arrange his schedule so he could still attend the enrichment co-op one afternoon a week. I think that speaks for itself.

Yes, huge learning went on, but it was the close-knit community of homeschoolers that resulted that gives this type of co-op my highest recommendation.

Teen-enrichment Co-op

When our extremely social youngest child was at home, and her siblings were off at college and university, we realized how lonely she felt. So I took it upon myself to start a co-op just for teenagers. I co-ran it for two years.

We put out a message to our local homeschooling network, and held an exploratory information and brainstorming session. We had no idea how many people would show up. Families representing twenty-five teens arrived at the meeting. Twenty-two of the teens ended up joining the Teen-enrichment Co-op. This was a great time for my daughter. She felt she had outgrown the other co-op, but she still desired interaction with other homeschooled teens.

This co-op ran from 10 a.m. to 2:30 p.m. every Friday for twelve weeks in the fall and winter. As we were drawing youth from across Ottawa and into Quebec, we wanted to avoid traffic. We ran this co-op similar to the multi-aged co-op except that the moms only had to teach one of the semesters, rather than both. As some of the moms still had other children at home, many wanted to drop off their children for the day. After my daughter went on to other things, I believe they came up with a different fee structure based on whether the child would be dropped off or the mom would stay to help.

One of the courses that was a huge hit was a course I created for the teens on how to land a volunteer or paid job position, from start to finish. This involved things like how to create a resume even if you had no job experience, where to find a position that was not advertised, and how to effectively handle interviews. The teens were fully engaged.

Instead of focusing on them as interview candidates, we explored the perspective of what the hiring manager's work-life might be like at the time they are conducting interviews. I found the teens came alive with an understanding of what that manager needed to see in a short 20-minute interview. I must say, I was so proud when a few of the students went home, applied what they had learned, landed an interview and were offered part-time jobs. I then had these individuals report back to the entire class on their actual process and what had worked for them.

Another class was a debating class wherein the students came up with topics to debate. They were often asked to take a stand for the opposite side. This taught them to see things from another's point of view—an excellent skill that could be applied to their eventual workplace.

This co-op structure provided teens with a forum set apart from the younger homeschooled children. This is an important consideration as teens often seek autonomy at this age. The classes were designed with this in mind, where teachers served more as facilitators.

Consider starting a teen homeschool co-op. Your teen will be ecstatic to learn that other homeschooled teens exist!

Two Family Co-op

Another co-op we ran involved my youngest daughter and one of her long-time friends who lived around the corner from us. Three mornings a week, the friend would walk over to our house, and I would teach the two of them writing. As we had a pool table, as long as they both stayed on task, they were allowed to have a game of pool at the end, before her friend returned home for lunch.

At first, the friend's mother and I were going to alternate months teaching. But after the first month, I told my friend that things were going so well, I did not mind continuing to do all of the teaching. We continued this for about seven months and more than covered the material we had planned for the entire year.

As my youngest sometimes struggles to stay on task, this simple co-op enabled her to achieve her writing goals while enjoying the company of a friend. In addition, it was rare she had to do any writing outside of the time allotted. This gave the other mom time to work with her other children. All in all, it was a win-win scenario.

Obviously, there are many types of co-ops. Some will fit your family better than others. I cannot stress enough the value we found from being involved in co-ops. My children often bring up some of the fun and crazy things they did in co-op. These shared experiences are what keep us close even today.

Co-ops are a fantastic way to meet the needs and ages of multiple children at varying stages of their development!

Chapter 8

WORK HARD AND PLAY HARD

I think sometimes it is so easy to get caught up in all the school work that needs to be done, that we forget to enjoy the freedoms we have in homeschooling. One of these key freedoms is the ability to build in playtime and plenty of it.

Super Hero Cape

When our son was learning to write, he struggled with spelling. To make the process a little more tolerable, I took a large piece of orange material that had somehow ended up in our dress-up box. Taking a thick permanent red marker, I drew two large "S" letters, side by side, in the center of it. After spelling, if he had tried his best—if he had worked through the list without complaining and without being defeated before trying—he would get to wear the Super Speller Cape and run all over the house like a superhero. This was a gigantic hit! The cape would flap behind him as he tore by and chanted that he was a super speller. I even kept a blind eye when he stood up on the living room couch, bounced a few times, and then leapt off and tore across the room. We did not have issues with spelling lessons after that.

Did he still struggle with spelling? Absolutely. Did he work hard at it most days? Yes. Was he awarded the cape every day? No. Usually, he would get to the end of spelling time and tell me his opinion on whether he thought he should wear the cape that day. I never disagreed with his assessment. He knew when he had tried his best. It was never about how many he got correct; it was always about whether he had done his personal best. I have no idea what happened to the super speller cape, but none of us has ever forgotten about it.

Think of one simple thing you can do to put the fun in your homeschooling.

Craft Cupboard

For many years we possessed a metal cupboard that had numerous shelves and a door. This became our craft cupboard. Inside it was stocked with all sorts of odds and ends, such as yarn, glue, tape, cardboard toilet paper rolls, scissors, pipe cleaners, stickers, swatches of material, wooden tongue depressors, cotton balls, beads, playdough, foil and interesting paper. This was a place where the children could go, and remove any of the items and construct anything they wanted out of it. They were never given any instructions on what they could make with the assorted objects.

During homeschooling, I would often allow them to sit at a table and construct things while I was reading to them. It also kept the youngest busy while the older two were still working through their schooling. Together they would sit and listen to the current book we were studying while their hands were busy constructing. At the end of a session on Ancient Rome, our son may have created a cardboard shaped aqueduct, one daughter may have fashioned a snake-shaped bracelet out of various beads and our other daughter might proudly hold up playdough versions of roman coins.

That craft cupboard was so well utilized, I was sure we were going to have to replace its door hinges. Often the children would be drawn to the contents of the craft cupboard long after the hours of schooling were complete. I did not empty this cupboard until my last child was all finished homeschooling.

Designate a shelf, cupboard or space for assorted odds and ends. Let the children decide what they create with its contents.

Change Your Medium

If your child is learning how to add and subtract, there is nothing to prevent you from letting him use a pencil on paper one day, a marker on a whiteboard the second day, or a piece of chalk on a driveway the next day.

The same goes for spelling exercises. They could be done orally one day, written down on a chalkboard the second day and on Fridays, be practiced through a game of Scrabble or Bananagrams.

If your child is writing a story or a poem, choose a time for him to stand up in front of his siblings and read it aloud.

Have each of them do this in turn. Then have them read it in a happy voice. The next time have them read it in a sad voice, an excited voice, or a scared voice.

Changing the medium can raise the enjoyment level of learning.

Impromptu Snow Day

One of the little things we did every year was agree to an impromptu snow day. This would occur on the first day it snowed enough that the entire lawn would be covered in delicious white snow. I say delicious because my youngest seemed to think it was the greatest thing to walk around with her tongue outstretched to capture the multi-shaped flakes. Our rule was that when this day landed, it did not matter what we had planned in terms of book work, the entire day would be spent outside playing in the snow. That meant all of us.

One of my fondest memories was when we were volunteering and living on-site at a farm that consisted of ten mowed acres and approximately 165 acres of forest. As soon as we saw the snow, we packed up hot dogs, marshmallows, trail mix, a large container of water and a steaming thermos of hot chocolate. Next, we put on our layers of pants, coats, scarves, mitts, hats and boots, and floated out the door into the winter wonderland.

Stopping to make snow angels along the way, we eventually reached our destination—a pit surrounded by stones and logs lying on their sides. Moving firewood and sticks into the centre, we soon had a raging fire. We spent five hours singing songs, playing in the snow and cooking over the fire. None of us had any desire to return home. It was one of those perfect days that will be forever etched in my memory.

Which days will be etched in your memories?

Impromptu Outings

One of my favourite things to do during the winter months was to suddenly tell my kids to close their books and come for lunch quickly because I was taking them to a matinee at the movie theatre. Where we live, theatres offer reduced rates on Tuesdays. Add to that an afternoon showing and the prices were even less. Sometimes we had the theatre to ourselves and other times there were no more than a dozen people present. Invariably one of us would remind the rest of us that everyone else was at school. Ah, the feeling of homeschooling freedom at its best!

To my children, these days were impromptu. To myself, they were a little more planned. I usually would try to gauge where they were in their studies for the week, taking account of their efforts and the last time we had an impromptu outing, as well as a general feeling that most of them—myself included—needed a break. So I might have this idea in my head a day or so in advance. Usually, I would not tell them until the day of the event. It just seemed to work better that way. I loved watching the delight on their faces.

If I decided to have an impromptu outing with my children and it happened to fall on the day that we would normally vacuum, dust—okay, I admit, we did not do that every week—or clean the bathrooms, we merely skipped these chores. Did we add these chores on to the next day? Absolutely not. We did not play catchup with chores. Instead, we left them for the following week during the regularly scheduled time. The only exception was that I might do a quick wipe down of the bathroom on the weekend. Everything else was left as it was.

Now, I will admit that trying not to cram chores into that day or the next one or two was extremely difficult for me initially. I am the type of person who likes things clean, neat and orderly. I am the person who does not tend to buy vacation souvenirs unless I know for sure I have a specific place to put them. I abhor clutter. When I am working, I have a difficult time getting things accomplished if my desk is messy and full of extraneous paper. So if you can relate to this, I understand how this may seem difficult. If you cannot relate to this, even better!

Not playing catch-up with chores removed a huge amount of stress. It provided us with the freedom to truly enjoy our time off—without being penalized because we had chores waiting for us when we arrived back home. Sure, it is entirely possible to head to the movies for a few hours and return home for chores before supper. But after the impromptu outing, we would often stop at a new park on the way home or the store for a birthday gift for a friend. Sometimes we would make hot chocolate and sit with our hands cupped around our warm mugs, while snuggled up on the couch discussing the show or outing together. Life is to be enjoyed and lived fully. These times with our children are precious.

Do not become a slave to chores and overburden yourself unnecessarily. Homeschooling affords this freedom. I hope you will take full advantage of it!

Public Swim and Skate Times

We took advantage of public swim and skate times. Family rates were incredibly reasonable during these daytime hours. It was always fun to go swimming indoors during those long winter days that seemed to stretch forever. The lifeguard at the pool always seemed very happy to see us. I believe we broke up the monotony of a slow afternoon.

What's a fun activity you can do with your children every month?

Showcase Your Children's Talents

Once or twice a year, we scheduled a visit to a senior's residence. We piggybacked off our homeschooling co-op and provided a sign-up sheet for one additional session to be held during the regularly scheduled time of the co-op. Each child could jointly or solo: dance, sing, perform illusion tricks, recite a poem, put on a simple skit or read a brief story they had written. This was a huge hit with the kids and the seniors. It also gave our children plenty of opportunities to speak in public, an invaluable life asset.

Find ways to showcase your children's gifts.

Museums and Special Exhibits

Our library system offers free passes for families to several museums and special exhibits in our city. These passes are in high demand and can take months to become available. I would request these passes online at the start of the school year. Whenever they arrived, they were valid for one week, so I would choose a day in that week to add an impromptu trip to the museum.

Over time, I realized that if we went after two o'clock in the afternoon, most of the school groups would be cleared out by then. Afterwards, the employees would be more than happy to give us personal tours and demonstrations. We took full advantage of these opportunities. As soon as I returned the passes to the library, I would go online and request them again. A few months later, we would be able to enjoy another free outing.

Many cities have museums that offer free times to visit during the week. I encourage you to check these out and take advantage of them as much as possible.

Foster a Healthy Work-life Balance Mentality

I think all of us can attest to the value of a healthy work-life balance, not just in our children's youth but well into their adult years. I expected my children to work hard and to do their best. At the same time, I wanted them to enjoy life. When our son was studying engineering at university, he would travel to school with my husband in the morning and return with him at the end of the day. When he was not in a class, he would work on his assignments.

Even with an incredible course load, multiple labs and a part-time job, it was very rare for my son to do any school-related work in the evenings or weekends. Working hard so that he had time to play was so ingrained in him that it surprised him when he heard of other students in his class scrambling to get their assignments completed despite feeling like all they did was study. This work-life balance has manifested itself in all three of my children. I believe it will serve them well as they marry and have families of their own.

What does a healthy work-life balance look like to you?

Plan an End of Unit or Year-end Party

I often have to be reminded by my husband to stop and celebrate the wins. I am the type of person that enjoys the journey but forgets to celebrate and quickly charges forward to the next exciting project. As a homeschooler, you have worked hard, and so have your children. Make sure to take time to celebrate!

One of the curriculums we used had us focus on the study of a particular period in time. We would read novels, write stories, and make and sample foods based on the time period. Thus at the end of the study, we would celebrate by dressing in the costumes of the time and serve the food that we had so carefully made together.

During one particular celebration, we decided we would have a theme representing Ancient Rome. We set crib mattresses on the tiled floor of the kitchen and used a large piece of wood for the table. We used bedsheets to dress in togas, and when my husband returned home from work, he was greeted with one as well. Then we sprawled out on the mattresses on the floor. Using our hands—the Romans did not use cutlery—we proceeded to devour the meatloaf that was formed into the shape of a roasted pig and stuffed with an apple. I thought it would have been an excellent time for the doorbell to have rung.

Remember to have some fun and to celebrate once in a while!

Chapter 9

BECOME A HOMESCHOOLING PROJECT MANAGER

One of my professional skills is project management. I honestly believe that if you implement a few key items from this discipline, it could take your homeschooling from mediocre to marvellous.

Define Your Vision

What is the goal of your homeschooling? Why do you homeschool? In an earlier chapter, I talked about finding data on homeschooling to which you can refer when you are feeling unmotivated or discouraged with home-schooling. But at all times, you need to know why you continue to homeschool. You need to have a vision. You need to have a why.

Initially, the thing that appealed to me about home-schooling was the freedom. Although I was an A student, I never liked school. I would read ahead in all of my subjects so that when I was at school, I could focus on socializing with my friends. I remember telling my dad that I had decided to go on and do a Masters degree directly following my undergraduate degree. He was floored. Not because he thought I could not handle it, but because he had heard me whine for years that I did not like school. I never understood why we had to sit for hours each day, and then go home and spend more time sitting doing homework. There was a huge world out there to explore, why would anyone spend so much of it sitting in a chair indoors?

When I discovered that homeschoolers on average fared better than public school kids, and that homeschoolers were regularly accepted into colleges and universities, I was sold. So, initially my why was the freedom it allowed. Yes, I wanted my kids to be educated. Homeschooling would achieve that while supporting an awesome way of life. For the first few years, that was my why.

Over time, there were so many serendipities of home-schooling that I felt like it was the best-kept lifestyle secret in the world. Focused, dedicated work time in the mornings followed by the freedom of afternoons, evenings and weekends to play and discover this amazing world God created, lured me in like a bear to honey.

So, on those days when things weren't going so well and nobody was motivated, I thought about our why. When my children were unmotivated, I reminded them of their whys. They were able to enjoy so much free time because they were homeschooled. I asked them to take a moment and think about what other kids in the neighbourhood were doing at that exact time. And they saw the why as well. In the business world, we call that the corporate vision. In homeschooling, we call it our homeschooling vision or more simply our why.

BECOME A HOMESCHOOLING PROJECT MANAGER

One of my closest friends is the most laidback person you would ever meet. She has a gift of hospitality, and making people feel relaxed and unburdened. I enjoy her company so much because she is never in a rush. I am sure if there were a fire in her house, she would be able to get everyone out calmly. This friend is not a morning person. Never was, never will be.

One of her current whys for homeschooling is that her day does not have to start at six, seven, eight or even nine a.m. I think her normal day starts at ten o'clock in the morning. So this is one of her why's. While in the early grades we were finished homeschooling well before lunch, her days might run into the mid or late afternoon. This works for her and her four children. Was this her original why? No. Does it add to her why now? Absolutely.

Another benefit of homeschooling is that we were able to take off on trips at any time of the year. My husband participated in annual information technology conferences as part of his work. These were perfect times to get away with him as the hotels were already covered. We usually would extend our stay so that my husband could enjoy a vacation as well. One time we were away twenty-three days. I had no idea the prices of amusement parks, tourist attractions and hotels varied so much. When you travel off-season, you can take advantage of drastically reduced rates and no line-ups. That became another one of our whys.

My children had the advantage of having both sets of grandparents living in the same city so they could see them any time they wanted. As my in-laws aged, they preferred meeting during the daytime. We had the flexibility to make that happen. Other times we would take off to spend lunch at my parents' house followed by a walk to their park for the afternoon. The freedom to be able to spend time with their grandparents, as much as they wanted, became another why.

You need a why. You need a big, fat, concrete why with several little ones all bound up with it. Homeschooling is an educational choice first, but ultimately, it is a lifestyle choice as well. I think it is important to determine all the positives that would disappear if you stopped home-schooling. But, you need to recognize these and remind yourself of yours. When I focused on all the amazing advantages our family enjoyed as a result of home-schooling, my energy and passion for homeschooling soared.

What are your reasons why? Post them on the fridge. Post them on the bathroom mirror. If your whys do not motivate you, you need to get a new why. Do it now. Do not wait another second. You need to remember your whys.

Define the How

A vision is fun, exciting and motivating if it is backed up by a how. How are we going to achieve our learning goals while enjoying a free lifestyle? This will not look the same for everyone, as it depends on your values, beliefs and priorities. You and your family need to decide what works for you. But hopefully in sharing our how, it will jumpstart a visual for you.

BECOME A HOMESCHOOLING PROJECT MANAGER

I like to think of our how in terms of a formula outlining how much time we would spend in each of four areas:

    ¼ Time on Academics
+ ¼ Time Spent Volunteering
+ ¼ Time Outdoors
+ ¼ Scheduled Downtime

= Positive Educational Lifestyle

Academics included things like Bible Study/devotions, math, reading, writing, English, physics etc. Yes, only one-quarter of our homeschooling time was spent on academics. This increased in the later years of high school, but not by much. If we were feeling bogged down in book work, it usually was because we had skewed our allotted times and were not spending enough time in the other areas.

Some people like to add chores to this schedule as it is definitely a life skill. Our children certainly had their fair share of chores, but I did not count it as part of their homeschooling routine. To me, it was a part of normal family responsibilities. By all means, go ahead and add it if that works better for you.

I have already spoken at length about volunteering. To be clear, the formula above is not necessarily a daily formula, but rather a weekly or bimonthly gauge to discern when we were off track.

Outdoor time was equated with exercise time. From hiking, biking, park hopping, roller-blading, skiing, trampolining, swimming to playing in the snow, we usually spent no less than two hours per day outside. Unless there was freezing rain or hail, you would find us outdoors. On certain days this might include dance courses or scouting activities.

The last element of our homeschooling formula I like to refer to as scheduled downtime. This was when there were no activities of any kind that you had to do. It was free time that was allocated during the weekdays. It never included electronics or television. I found that if this downtime was not scheduled in, it did not happen. Without downtime, our attitudes would suffer, our motivation would decrease, and our stress levels would skyrocket. That certainly did not equate to a healthy way of life.

Our son needed and craved more downtime than our girls. He is an introvert by nature, so it was important to him to have enough solitary time to recharge his batteries. Our homeschooling formula helped us to ensure this happened.

Today, we have three extremely capable, creative and resourceful children who understand what delineates a healthy work-life balance. I attribute this to actively scheduling enough down-time. When you are feeling rushed, and activities you love feel like a chore, it is time to take a good look at where you are spending your time.

After explaining our homeschooling formula to others, invariably I have been questioned on how we were able to spend only a quarter of our time on academics and still complete everything we set out to do. First of all, one must remember that there is no commute time to and from school, explanations of work are for a few students only, difficulties or questions are handled immediately, school start time is scheduled early in the morning, and my children could move on as soon as concepts were mastered. Combined, these advantages of homeschooling enabled us to complete academic work in a timely manner—a manner that is not readily available to those in the traditional school setting.

How much weight do you give to each of the components of your homeschooling equation? How much do you want to give? What can you change to achieve this?

Implement Continuous Improvement

I will not claim that we had everything figured out in the first year or two of homeschooling. It took us some time to evaluate and make changes. Sometimes this involved tweaking a few things, other times it meant instituting completely new processes and procedures. Formally, this was a yearly process.

When I was a project manager, we always conducted a detailed post mortem at the close of a project. This was not something I did in isolation. Every person involved in the project was invited to discuss what went well, what did not, and offer suggestions on how we could improve for the next project. The key was to learn from our experiences so that to the best of our combined abilities, the next project would run even more smoothly. We would keep what worked well and change what did not work to continuously improve the process.

In homeschooling, at the close of the year, we would have a celebration day and leave it at that. No one wanted to talk about the next year because they were elated school was over. But, during the first few days of the new homeschooling year, I would sit down with my children and help them plan out the year. We talked about what they needed to achieve that year and how they were going to do it. We reflected on what worked well the previous year and where we needed to make changes.

The most important part of those discussions was that my children played a huge role in the scheduling. My older two wanted to work really hard the first three days of the week and then schedule co-ops, outings etcetera at the end of the week. In addition, they focused on completing all of their daily studies at the start of the day before engaging in volunteer, outdoor or scheduled downtime activities.

My youngest had a very difficult time working straight through, so she liked to intersperse her days between work and play. At first, I was reluctant, but as she reminded me, it was her schedule and as long as the work got done, she should be able to set her own schedule. I could not argue with that. As such, she would often be found late at night working on her school work. Even today, at university, she will work on her assignments every day, as she is not a crammer who leaves things to the last moment, but many of her assignments are done late at night. She schedules her classes so that she can sleep in in the mornings. This works best for her.

At the end of each week, it was easy to gauge if someone was falling behind. We would discuss why this was and come up with a game plan to fix it. Sometimes schedules were rejigged, other times it just meant that a particular section took more time and it would be added to the following week. If they did not put in the time and effort required, they would have to get it done on the weekend. No one wanted to work on the weekend, so this was a rare occurrence. I never taught on the weekend. Our goal was always to do your best and focus on mastering the material before moving forward.

Brooke, my youngest, enjoys listening to music while she is working. When she consistently met her study goals, I had to stop questioning this arrangement. When she could not stay still to work through her math sheet, we acquired a large exercise ball that she could sit on while situated in front of her desk. Her ability to focus increased. I wish I had trusted her judgement earlier. I believe it would have alleviated some of our frustration with each other. But over time, as we discussed what was working and what was not, and tried out new things, we were able to increase how often we found mutually agreeable solutions. As a result, our relationship improved dramatically.

By including my children in the planning—and as they got older, allowing them to set their own schedules—they were more apt to keep up a consistent pace of learning. The key point is that planning always involved a discussion of what worked the year before, what did not and creative ways we could change things. Because they were involved in this process, they owned their schedules, making them more apt to follow through on commitments. I found this to be so important in the late pre-teen and teen years.

Ensure your children are involved in the planning, implementation and evaluation phases of homeschooling.

Be genuinely open to their suggestions. You may be surprised at the results!

Change Your Curriculum

There are some good curriculums and there are some fabulous curriculums. These may not be classified as such for each of your children. If something is not working, change it. I remember in grade two that my son was so frustrated with the repetitive math sheets. He did not understand why he had to repeat worksheet after worksheet on addition that he already knew and understood.

If Kent was already bored and frustrated in grade two, what would he be like in grade five? He assimilated mathematics very easily. Once he got it, he needed to move on. I went to my homeschooling network and sought out those who loved their math curriculums. As I mentioned before, over a weekend, I borrowed one of my friend's video-based math programs and watched numerous hours of video. The next year we bought the program and were thrilled with it.

When Brooke started studying high school English, I admit I was bored with the material because I had used it with my other two. In addition, she had been around while they were studying some of the books that we were reading out loud together, so she felt like she had already covered some of the material. We went online and searched for recommended books for her grade level and beyond. We requested these items from the library and were both thrilled when we were able to delve into new material together.

Change your curriculum. Learning does not have to be boring for either your children or you!

Chapter 10

PUT YOUR MIND AT EASE

One thing I have found that many homeschool parents do, is that they wonder if they are doing a good job. They worry if their children will learn everything they need to learn to get into college, university or a trade school. They fret over whether they will complete all of their workbooks over the course of a year. They agonize over whether their children will ever learn to read and write. I know that home-schooling parents do this because I definitely did this! The fact that I took on the responsibility for the education of my children, meant that if things did not go well or turn out well, it was going to be my fault.

The purpose of this chapter is to totally and fully put your mind at ease. If you love your children and you are actively homeschooling to the best of your ability, then you do not have to worry. There are many reasons why this is the case.

Focus on the Reality

With access to information that we now have at our fingertips, everything one would ever want to know or learn is completely accessible. If your child learns to read well, write well and acquires a solid understanding of basic mathematics, then they can learn anything.

Our son struggled to learn to read. He might see the word 'the' three times in the same sentence, and even though I would tell him what the word was, it was as if he had forgotten it when it popped up again in the next sentence. This would repeat itself when he came across it in the fourth, fifth and sixth sentences. We worked at learning to read every day and we sought out the resources that worked for him.

When our son reached grade six, it was a huge strain for him to write a sentence beyond a grade two or three level. I remember sitting down with him and telling him that God had given him an incredible brain. It enabled him to design, build and create things so beyond other children his age. It allowed him to understand the concepts of things that many people did not contemplate until university. But, I then explained to him that because God had wired his brain this way, it meant that other things that were easy for other people were difficult for him. I explained to him that it did not matter if writing was difficult and that it took so much time, as long as he worked at it, he would get better.

At the same time, I researched writing programs and found one that suited him. It helped him advance, but he still had to work very hard at it to make progress. I remember one particular day being very upfront with him and saying that it did not matter if it was difficult, it did not matter if it took him extra time, he still had to learn to write—and write well. We talked about how inventors and engineers could have the best ideas in the world, but if they could not effectively communicate to others what these amazing ideas were, no one would ever know about them. Something changed in him that day. It's like he suddenly accepted that if he worked at it in small bits every day, he would get better and better. He no longer complained. He just spent the time and got it done.

A few years ago, Kent came home from university and told me he had received his marks for the previous semester in engineering. There was one, in particular, he wanted me to see. He watched my face as I scanned the transcript and then looked back up at him—he's 6'2" and I am 5'4". We both broke out in a huge grin at the same time. He had managed to get an A in his Writing for Engineers course. Yes, he had done extremely well in all of his classes, but he and I both agreed that that mark was his greatest victory!

As I sit here in my home office, putting the final touches on *The Happy Homeschooler*, Kent is working across the hall from me. He is working on the final version of a presentation that he will deliver next week at a technical conference on a software tool that he created. His company is flying him from Ottawa to California to share his innovative tool with others in the industry. I am bursting with pride because I know what it took for him to get to this point!

Do not get caught up in adding subject upon subject. Focus on reading, writing and math to start; these are essential. As your children master those, go on to the other subjects. If they work at it every day, the reality is that they will get better over time.

Teachers Rarely Cover Entire Textbooks

It came as a great surprise to me to learn that teachers rarely cover all the chapters in a textbook. So as long as you are moving forward, do not fret if you have put the time in and cover only seventy or eighty per cent of the material. If your child studies biology at university and he took it back in grade nine or ten, there is a good chance he will not remember all of the material anyway. The same goes for geography, science, history, chemistry, physics, English etc.

The only exception to this is mathematics; as I said before it builds upon itself. Instead, do not worry that you do not finish it in a particular year, simply pick it up the following year and continue from where you left off. It should never be about grade level; it should be about mastery.

Nowhere does it state that every chapter of every book needs to be completed in its entirety.

No Parent Knows Every Subject

I was gifted with a very logical brain, so I tend to excel in math and science. Additionally, I am a visual learner. The area I struggle with is in learning languages. This is very difficult for me and was so apparent when my daughter and I were taking Karate lessons together. The calls for the moves were all in Japanese. It did not seem to matter how many times they were repeated in class, I would still have trouble deciphering them, which would almost always lead to me being a step behind the entire class.

Not surprisingly, the one area that I felt inadequate in teaching my children were languages. So for these subjects, we used audio and video-based programs. My son enjoys Japanese cartoons and has watched so many that he now understands Japanese. I would never have guessed as he was the one who struggled for years with reading and writing.

Each of my children has pursued very different fields of study— engineering, music and business. When they have a passion for something, they take the necessary steps to learn about it. Your job is to help them learn how to learn. You do not have to know everything, nor do you have to teach them everything. Over time, they will teach themselves. This may happen when they are merely eleven years old, like our middle daughter. Or it may happen for some of their subjects and not others initially. Rest assured, their gifts will show themselves. Their passions will immerge. They will be okay.

Do not worry where you fall short. Your children will naturally pick up the things that interest them.

Homeschooling is Like Having a Tutor

When children struggle to learn at a traditional school, the teacher may not be aware until a test. Often the child will fall behind because the teacher has to move forward to cover all of the material required by the Ministry of Education. Often at this point, the teacher might suggest a parent hire a private tutor for their child.

The one-on-one of homeschooling is equal to your children having a tutor at their disposal twenty-four seven. You know as soon as they are having issues and need more help or when they easily master the material and can skip over pages of repetitive exercises. Overall the chances of your children learning are much better than that of being in a class full of twenty to thirty students.

Homeschooling has similar benefits to having a private tutor.

There are Many Opportunities to Develop Cherished Character Traits

I always marvel when I hear parents say they are so glad that the summer break is over and their children are back in school. It is like they feel a huge relief. I know I needed a break from time to time, but being together so much teaches your children not to give up on relationships, but rather, to work through the difficulties and personality differences, to continually get along. It is not okay to avoid each other, or bully each other, or put each other down. It is required that you say you are sorry when you do something wrong, ask for forgiveness when you mess up and treat each other with respect. Public school does not always afford this in unsupervised settings, such as in the playground, hallways or on the bus.

When your children are still learning what acceptable behaviours are, and they are still developing, you have control over their environments. Because you are together all the time, you and they need to keep working on relationships. This will serve them well when they have their own families and they go off to pursue their careers.

We valued integrity, accountability, responsibility and respect. Homeschooling gave us a plethora of opportunities to discuss and practice these character traits. This, in itself, makes homeschooling such a valuable educational choice for your children.

Consider the Worst-case Scenario

What if things do not go as well as you were hoping? Perhaps your child will take an extra year to finish school, or he does not meet all the requirements to enter a particular program at college or university. This happens to kids in school all the time. Some go back for an extra year at high school—a victory lap; others take online courses in the summer to make up for courses they need, while others work jobs until they figure out what they want to do. Nothing is preventing your children from doing the same.

How many people definitively know what they want to do in life? It can take some time to figure this out. Think of how many times people change jobs in their lives. Homeschooling will not put your children at any more of a disadvantage than kids in the regular school system.

Even if your children have learning disabilities, do not be so quick to assume that the regular school will be able to give them everything they need in terms of extra help and resources. Clearly, do everything to help your children to advance, but do not beat yourself up if they are weak in certain areas.

Homeschooling is a great choice. In fact, homeschooling is a fabulous choice! The data proves it. You love your child more than someone who is teaching them at school. Have faith that your love, support and devotion will be enough. It is more than enough!

And Now it is Your Turn

I truly hope that if you have made it this far in this book, you have found some concrete examples of ways to improve your homeschooling. I hope you are feeling the excitement of how great homeschooling can be when certain strategies are put into practice.

The title of each chapter in *The Happy Homeschooler* utilizes a verb to indicate that each of the ten strategies involves taking a specific action or actions to bring about some positive change in your homeschooling journey. Yes, you need to actively do something to provide a catalyst for change. Please do not feel you have to implement everything! Choose the things that appeal to you and fit with your goals and aspirations for you and your family.

If you have found several things you want to change, do not feel you have to implement them all at once. The last thing you want to do is cause unnecessary overload or the feeling of being overwhelmed. Choose one or two things that resonated with you and implement those. Once they are in place, add something else. Over a short period, I assure you your homeschooling joy will rise to new and exciting heights. Even just a few actions can have significant positive results! If you would like to receive a FREE GIFT to help you prioritize the actions you want to implement to become a Happy Homeschooler, you can access this FREE GIFT via my website at traceyhagerman.com.

I loved homeschooling, and for the majority of the time they were in the throws of it so did my children. I believe that joy carried over to other people as I sat over many, many cups of tea and shared our homeschooling experiences. Professionally, I helped organizations and individuals manage significant change, and I always delighted in seeing the result after an intervention. It is amazing how tweaking a few key areas of your homeschooling can make a tremendous difference. My prayer for you is that you too will feel that heavenly joy that is possible in homeschooling, even when your children struggle, things do not go as planned and the chores loom in the background. Yes, I do believe in homeschooling heaven, because we lived it!

In recent years, I sat down with each of my children and asked them if they felt that homeschooling had been a good choice for them. In all three cases, it was a resounding, yes! Many of their insights have been included in this book.

Now that we are on the other side of homeschooling, I must say that each time I pass a park, I visualize my children and I playing on the swings. Tears come to my eyes as I thank God for granting me the amazing privilege to have home educated my children. I feel blessed to have had a wonderful husband who supported this decision wholeheartedly. I treasure the memories of all the things our family did together. This includes the tough times, the fun times and everything else in between because it means we made it through together and we are closer for it. I would not have wanted it any other way.

Homeschooling is an incredible way of life. Do not let anyone or anything steal your joy! You can do this! May your journey be a fruitful one! May you truly be a Happy Homeschooler!

ACKNOWLEDGEMENTS

No novel comes together without the help of an amazing team of people. Thank you to my incredible husband Jonathon for providing encouragement, support and unwavering belief in this project.

A heartfelt thank you to Liane Smith, who provided valuable insights and suggestions that greatly improved the final version.

A huge thank you to Bernice Martin Delcorde, whose editing skills, once again enabled me to produce a reader friendly book. Thanks for sticking with me as I moved into the world of non-fiction.

A giant thank you to my book formatter, Jen Henderson. I appreciate the way you transformed my file into a professional looking book!

If you would like to receive a **FREE** download to help you prioritize the actions you want to implement to become a Happy Homeschooler, you can request this **FREE** resource at traceyhagerman.com.

If you would like to book a speaker for your upcoming homeschooling conference, podcast, or virtual event please feel free to contact me via my website at traceyhagerman.com. A comprehensive list of suggested seminar topics is available on my website. It always gives me so much joy to share the wonderful world of homeschooling with you and your loved ones. I love meeting so many fascinating homeschoolers!

If you enjoyed this book and would like to read other books by Tracey Hagerman, you can check them out at traceyhagerman.com.

Made in the USA
Middletown, DE
05 August 2021